On Rousseau

KEY CRITICAL THINKERS IN EDUCATION
Volume 3

Series Editors:

Michael A. Peters
University of Illinois at Urbana-Champaign, USA

Tina (A.C.) Besley
California State University, San Bernardino, USA

Scope:

This series is an edition dedicated to the revival of the critical approaches of key thinkers whose thought has strongly influenced and shaped educational theory: Rousseau, Marx, Gramsci, Dewey, Marcuse, Rogers, Freire, Derrida, Foucault, Said and Butler. In this first edition the series includes eleven monographs in total, each approximately sixty pages long with three chapters, a brief introduction, a bibliographical essay, a glossary and series of study questions. The aim is designed to provide cheap and accessible texts for students that give clear accounts of these thinkers and their significance for educational theory. The monographs are written by a group of internationally renown scholars whose own work embodies the critical ethos.

On Rousseau

An Introduction to his Radical Thinking on Education and Politics

Kenneth Wain
University of Malta, Malta

SENSE PUBLISHERS
ROTTERDAM/BOSTON/TAIPEI

A C.I.P. record for this book is available from the Library of Congress.

ISBN: 978-94-6091-383-9 (paperback)
ISBN: 978-94-6091-384-6 (hardback)
ISBN: 978-94-6091-385-3 (e-book)

Published by: Sense Publishers,
P.O. Box 21858,
3001 AW Rotterdam,
The Netherlands
www.sensepublishers.com

Printed on acid-free paper

DEDICATION

For
Dylan and Lori

TABLE OF CONTENTS

INTRODUCTION

Introducing Rousseau

"It is too difficult to think nobly when one thinks for a living. If one is to have the strength and the courage to speak great truths one must not depend on one's success."

(Rousseau, The Confessions completed 1770, first published 1781)

EMILE IN CONTEXT

Jean-Jacques Rousseau is best known in the world of education for his famous book *Emile or On Education* (1762b). More usually referred to as *Emile* the book has been universally regarded as an education classic: "one of those rare total or synoptic books ... comparable to Plato's *The Republic*, which it is meant to rival or supersede," (Bloom, 1979:1991, pp. 3–4) and "a seminal book" for the modern theory of education. (Rusk, 1918:1979, p. 100) Hence, not surprisingly, most of what has been written about Rousseau and education is about *Emile* virtually disregarding the rest of his writing on the subject. Indeed, his writing on education began well before he even started writing *Emile*, which was in 1758. His first thoughts on the subject appear very much earlier and in a much shorter work, the *Project for the Education of M. de Saint-Marie* written in 1740 after a short period of time when he tried his hand, unsuccessfully, at being a family tutor. A decade later in the *Discourse on the Sciences and Arts* (henceforth the *First Discourse*), published in 1750, we find his first critical remarks on the current state of education in his society. The link of education with politics established with this his very first political work, was to subsist consistently in his later thinking. It is not very visible, however, to the reader who confines her interest in Rousseau to the reading of *Emile* (particularly if that interest is further limited to the early parts of the book that have most influenced modern pedagogical practices). With readers of this kind, who tend to be typical in the world of education, the link is mostly unnoticed, and with it the writing on education that stems directly from his political work tends to be ignored also.

Significant among the latter is his work about the political role that institutions of public instruction, namely public schools, should play in society, and about the state's stake in such institutions. These were topics first addressed in an article on *Political Economy* which he wrote for Volume 5 of the *Encyclopaedia* and published in 1755 and which subsequently appeared as an independent essay in 1758 under the name *Discourse on Political Economy* (henceforth the *Third Discourse*). Many years later, in 1771, we find him taking up the same subject again in *Considerations on the Government of Poland* (henceforth *Poland*, published posthumously). These writings about public schooling, however, do not exhaust the list of other educational writings besides *Emile*. There are important pedagogical passages in *Julie or the New Heloise* (henceforth *Heloise*), published in 1761, that anticipate *Emile* and that are often passed over by readers and commentators despite their intrinsic interest. *Heloise* and *Emile* were designated by Rousseau himself as novels, though today's reader would find little in them that would identify them as such. *Heloise* is also a book about domestic education, another dimension of his writing on education which is not found in *Emile*, and which is politically relevant also in its own right. Book Five of *Emile* is about the education of women. Then there is a part late in Book Four, named the 'Profession of Faith of a Savoyard Vicar' on self-education. Gabriel Compayre, an early twentieth century commentator on *Emile* dismissed it out of hand as "somewhat of a digression in an educational treatise," and remarked that it has "small value" as "a philosophical work." (1908:2002, p. 46) But Rousseau regarded it as the most significant part of *Emile* capable of standing alone as a separate book in its own right, to the extent that he entrusted it to the keeping of his surest friends when he thought the manuscript as a whole was in danger.

We are really only interested here in the first of these judgments, but Compayre is mistaken in both. Given the great importance we know that Rousseau attached to the subject of religious education his thoughts on the subject cannot be described as marginal to his thoughts about education in general, even less as "a digression" from them. With regards the *Profession*'s philosophical value, Rousseau himself insisted that his philosophical thinking was very close to the Vicar's. "The result of my arduous research," he says towards the end of his life, "was more or less what I have written in my 'Profession of Faith of the Savoyard Vicar'." (1776b:1979, p. 55) And Judith Shklar has remarked that although they are not strictly identical the Vicar's views are fairly close to Rousseau's. (Strong 2002, p. 125) A third way of reading the *Profession* is as an account of a project of self-education; what Rousseau refers to as his "arduous research." From this point of view it features as still another dimension of Rousseau's writing on education, usually unnoticed, besides that of the family and the citizen. Finally, to complete our list of his contributions to education Nicholas Dent has described his *Moral Letters*, written in 1757–58 for Sophie d'Houdetot, namely in the same period as *Heloise*, as an educational work "loosely defined," because though they are not "truly intended as sources of guidance and instruction," their didactic tone is unmistakable and also echo themes in *Emile*. (2005, p. 24)

WRITING ABOUT ROUSSEAU

Emile was written almost concurrently with his political classic *On the Social Contract* (henceforth *Social Contract*) published a month before it in April 1762. Between the *First* and *Third Discourse* Rousseau wrote the *Discourse on the Origin of Inequality* first published also in 1755 (henceforth the *Second Discourse*), also regarded as a classic of political philosophy. In Chapter One I shall discuss these political works, together with *Poland*, in relation to his interests in education. Rousseau, an autodidact himself, wrote on a variety of other subject besides politics and education; on music, language, the theatre, religion, botany, and so on, and his writing was always controversial – and this includes *Emile*. He entered into frequent, often very bitter, polemics of different sorts with his contemporaries on these subjects. He was charged by them with desultory writing and disconnected thinking, his work dismissed as a body of "fatuous declamations, adorned with fine language but disconnected and full of contradictions." Accusations he strenuously rejected, repeatedly defending the integrity of his work as a consistent project, "profoundly thought out, forming a coherent system ... which offered nothing contradictory." (1776a:1990, p. 209)

What order should we follow in discussing these works in our commentary on his thinking on education? I have set aside Dean Rusk's advice to begin with *Poland*, Rousseau's last contribution to the subject. Rusk reverses the historical order of Rousseau's writing arguing in self-defence that this accords with "a natural and logical order." (1918:1979, p. 105) He does not explain why he regards *Poland* a natural or logical beginning nor do I know what he means in this context. I do not myself believe that there is any natural or logical way of writing about any author never mind one like Rousseau who was constantly defending himself from critics who dismissed his works as disordered and illogical. If we look at Rousseau's own wish on the matter, we find it in the mouth of the 'Frenchman' in *Rousseau Judge of Jean-Jacques: Dialogues*, his last but one substantial work completed in 1776 close to the end of his life and, like most of his later work, published posthumously (henceforth the *Dialogues*) that he wanted his work to be read in "the reverse of their order of publication." This would seem to vindicate Rusk, but Rousseau was thinking not of *Poland* but of *Emile* as his last published work (and so it was). *Emile* was, by his estimation, the culmination of his literary labours and was intended to bring them to a conclusion. (1776a:1990, p. 211) The writings that followed after were "destined only to the personal defence of his homeland and his honour." (p. 211) *Poland*, in this sense, was a one off, a work written against a commission.

On my part, I have decided that the safest way to go about writing this short introductory work (not necessarily unnatural or illogical either) is to follow, more or less, the historical order of his writing from the *First Discourse* on and leading up to his trilogy of masterpieces on politics and education, *Heloise*, *Emile* and the *Social Contract* – the last mentioned I also read as a work of this kind. Although there is nothing mentioned directly about education in it, it is concerned with the education of the citizen and conceives the state itself as an educational agency. I have put *Poland* in Chapter One and discussed it together with the *Third Discourse* as, in a sense, a practical attempt to put the principles of state education which he had explored in the earlier work in a specific national context. Chapter Two begins with a discussion of *Heloise* which he started shortly before *Emile*. A discussion on *Emile* itself follows in the same chapter which also includes Rousseau's views about the education of women and the Vicar's project of self-education referred to earlier. Chapter Three, the concluding chapter, is mainly a historical/political/ pedagogical evaluation of *Emile* and its author, of their influence on modern education and their significance today. A Rousseau biography runs through all the chapters together with the commentary and sets the biographical context for the works discussed.

READING ROUSSEAU

The biographical context is important in Rousseau's case. As Tracy Strong has remarked about him; his "books do not lend themselves to be understood ... unless one understands their author." (2002, p. 12) And this, indeed, is nothing more than what Rousseau himself declared. Maurice Cranston who has written a detailed three-volume biography of Rousseau adds that "it is a commonplace that Rousseau's writings, more than those of most authors, need to be read in the context of his life." (1983, p. 10) My concurrence with this thinking explains why I chose not just to distribute his biography over the book (rather than confine it briefly to the pages of the introduction) but also to give it the generous space it occupies in the book. Like most other of his biographies mine depends substantially on his own auto-biographical writing, on *The Confessions* (1770) especially, but also on the unfinished *Reveries of the Solitary Walker* (henceforth *Reveries*) and the *Dialogues*. In several places in these works, Rousseau relates his writing with personages and episodes in his own life. Thus, for instance, he reads himself to a considerable degree in the character of St Preux, Julie's tutor in *Heloise*, and is the unknown young man receiving the Vicar's (a character himself based on two priests who had influenced his life in his own youth) advice in *Emile*. The character named 'Rousseau' in the *Dialogues* says to the 'Frenchman' about Jean-Jacques (the subject of the dialogue, namely Rousseau himself) "I find in him today the features of Emile's Mentor. Perhaps in his youth I would have found those of St Preux." (1776a:1990, p. 90)

Dent (2005), Cranston (1983), and Matthew Simpson (2007), and others have suggested that his work can be profitably divided into three phases corresponding with his age and the changing circumstances of his life and personality; the three commentators differ only in the time bands and in the titles they give to each phase. Dent dates the first and earliest phase between 1712 and 1749 and refers to it as Rousseau's 'apprentice' years. This was a time when his interests lay principally in the arts and he wrote musical, literary, and theatrical works, *and* scholarly works on music and language, and when his political ideas and agenda were still in the process of forming (Simpson, 'Youth', 1712–1742, Cranston, 'Early Life and Work', 1712–1754). I follow Dent who I take to have picked 1749 because it was *the* defining year for Rousseau. As we shall see, it signalled a radical change in his interests, outlook, and way of life. The second phase Dent refers to as 'mature' and marks between 1750 and 1764, the years when Rousseau produced his best writing in politics and education. This phase, however, effectively reached its culmination in 1762 with the publication of *Emile*, as Simpson and Cranston hold. (Simpson, 'Ascendancy', 1742–1762, Cranston, 'The Noble Savage', 1754–1762). It opened with the writing of the *First Discourse* and encompassed the peak years of his writing that produced the masterpieces for which he has remained famous and that are our chief concern in this book; his three *Discourses*, the *Social Contract*, *Heloise*, and *Emile*. Finally, the years until his death in 1778 were years of 'decline', of retreat and solitude, blighted by paranoia about a grand plot against him by his erstwhile friends, all bent in his mind on his persecution and destruction. (Simpson, 'Retreat':1762–1778, Cranston, 'The Solitary Self': 1762–1778). Rousseau's writings in this phase, *The Confessions*, the *Dialogues*, a pamphlet *To All*

Frenchmen ..., written also in 1776 just after the *Dialogues*, culminating in his last work the *Reveries*, also started in the same year but left unfinished at his death, were mainly confessional and autobiographical and intended for his self-vindication and for the sake of posterity.

WHY READ ROUSSEAU?

What Rousseau's autobiographies offered his reader, as he says himself, was his candid self-disclosure. What he sought from his reader in return was "a direct and unmediated response to his writing," an unbiased reading uninfluenced by the voices of his hostile critics, (Strong, 2007, p. 8) a 'friendly' ear. (Reisert, 2003) Why, however, should one listen at all to Rousseau today? Several answers could be suggested. One could easily be intrigued by his controversial and in many ways tragic life and personality, for instance. Or perhaps because we still find him relevant today! It "could be that Rousseau, whether telling us of our history or of his condition, whether examining the social contract or writing his confessions, illuminates one of the deep enduring themes that troubles both our social thought and our social practice – the relationship between individual and community," as one writer has suggested. (Gauthier, 2006, p. 4) Put slightly differently, he may be relevant to us because he

> "(...) addresses each of his readers personally because he addresses the concerns, small and great, that each of us must confront for ourselves, in our daily existence. He writes about the everyday challenges of the moral life, about how hard it can be to live up to our own ideals, and about what steps we can take in order to live happier and better lives. He writes about the everyday challenges of our living together in political community, about the difficulty of preserving our freedom, both from the powerful, institutional forces that threaten to overwhelm us from the outside and from our vices that threaten to destroy our liberty from within." (Reisert, 2003, p. ix)

In short, because his concerns are still ours, yours and mine, and because he "addresses these concerns – my concerns – with passion and intensity, as if they matter more than anything else in the world." (p. ix) And what are these concerns about the politics of existence if not also concerns about education?

When the question of *Emile*'s relevance was being discussed, as it periodically has continued to be, just over a century ago, at the time when his fame was slowly growing again after years of virtual neglect, Compayre referred to "forgotten recesses" in the book where, as he put it, "lurk more than one reflection which, hitherto unperceived, proves to be fruitful in instruction for the people of our time, and directly suited to their present requirements." (1908:2002, p. 4) It is a moot point whether this remark is still significant today; whether any such 'recesses' still remain after so many readings and depredations from the book by followers and critics. One wonders whether the archive of pedagogical reflections for educators one finds in the book is not now exhausted and whether we should not simply declare it as beyond its sell-by date for educators and their practice. Compayre declared that "*Emile* deserves to remain the eternal object of the educator's medita-tion, were it only because it is an act of faith and trust in humanity." (p. 5)

But is it an act of faith and trust in humanity? Allan Bloom, much more recently (1978), and also a sympathetic voice, says yes. He insists, like David Gauthier (2006) and Joseph Reisert (2003) whom I have just quoted, that *Emile* still speaks to and "of a real world of which we all have experience, no matter what our language," i.e. he agrees that the book is immortal, and that reading it stretches the horizons of our understanding of human possibility. (p. vii) It is a book, Bloom says, "with which one can live and which becomes deeper as one becomes deeper," (p. 3) even if, he remarks, it "has little appeal to contemporary taste." (p. vii) As a teacher, reading it still provokes him, he says, to consider his practices and his pedagogical philosophy. It gives one a "new sense of what it means to be a teacher and of the peculiar beauty of the relationship between teacher and student," and could still, for that reason, be held up today as a pedagogical example. (p. ix) But is he right? Is there truly a beautiful relationship between teacher and student described in *Emile* that should inspire teachers universally and for all time? Can one advise teachers today to adopt the tutor in *Emile* as their model? These are questions that will be returned to in Chapter Three, when they will be addressed specifically. There are other questions that will also need to be taken up in that chapter and in earlier ones. Rousseau was, if nothing, as I remarked briefly earlier, a controversial and often paradoxical personality and thinker. This makes him difficult to place; was he conservative or progressive, an early democrat or a deeply totalitarian thinker? What is his relation to the modern world, what has been his influence on it? We know that he aroused strong passions in his society both for and against him, and that the controversy has never ceased though the passions may long have dampened so that there are still contrary evaluations of his works today as there have ever been.

Bloom, a conservative critic, whose famous translation of *Emile* I am using in this book, is among the more sympathetic of his commentators. "A latter-day representative of the natural rights doctrines of Rousseau," as he has been referred to, he even favours some of the more hotly contested of Rousseau's views; on the role of women and the family, for instance, subjects still very much contended over today, views that, to the contrary, irk his progressive critics, women more generally, feminists in particular, and liberal-minded men also. (Spring, 1994, p. 114) Rousseau himself always described his work as didactic; as dedicated to revealing to his readers the source of human error and prejudice and to indicating to them "the route to true happiness," back to their hearts where they could "rediscover the seeds of social virtue" stifled by the so-called progress of their societies. (1776b:1990, p. 22) Is this call still relevant today? Some have described him as a modern thinker, even the first. His educational thought has been described as championing children's rights and inspiring child-centred pedagogies. Others have questioned his more general commitment to freedom, and described him as anti-social and obsessed with the solitary individual. These contrary readings are explored in this book. But first, his early biography.

FORMATIVE YEARS 1712–1749

1.–1741

Jean-Jacques Rousseau was born on June 28, 1712 in Geneva, the second son of Isaac a master watchmaker, member of the select class of highly skilled artisans in the city, and a citizen, and Suzanne Bernard, a Calvinist pastor's daughter of higher breeding. Geneva at the time was "a sombre fortress ruled by the austere, repressive ethos of Calvinism. And yet it was a city with good grounds for pride, for it was a centre of culture and learning, and had a long history of political autonomy," with the citizens enjoying civil liberties unknown in most of the Europe of the time. (Cranston, 1983, p. 14) Suzanne died of puerperal fever on 7 July soon after his birth, aged thirty-nine, leaving him "almost dead," and with a tragic legacy to bear for his life, "the seed of a disorder which has grown stronger with the years." (1770:1953, p. 19) Isaac raised him with the help of a nurse and an aunt also named Suzanne whose singing to him influenced his lifelong passion for music.

His early childhood was spent reading his mother's novels with his father, from where, he says, he acquired his earliest knowledge of the human passions. Then they turned to the serious part of her library; diverse histories and classics, among them Plutarch's *Lives* which remained his "favourite" for life. (1776b:1979, p. 63) He was not allowed out to play with other children of his age, a factor that denied him a "true childhood" and deeply influenced his later writing of *Emile*. He was, he says, a "prodigy" who "always felt and thought like a man." (1770:1953, p. 67) To his father he later attributed his "strongest passion," of patriotism, a "proud and intractable spirit," and an "impatience with the yoke of servitude," which marked his life and influenced all his political and educational thinking. (p. 20) He also followed his father in being "scrupulously upright, and most religious," but also "pleasure-loving." (p. 66) One day in 1722, Isaac got involved in a violent quarrel with a Captain Gautier and had to flee the city to avoid arrest, abandoning Jean-Jacques and his older brother Francois in the process.

His maternal uncle Gabriel Bernard took them both in his charge, apprenticed the latter, and put Jean-Jacques and his own son, roughly his age, in a boarding school in the neighbouring village of Bossey run by a Pastor Lamberciere and his thirty year old sister. There Rousseau received the only formal schooling of his life at the hands of Lamberciere, "a very intelligent man" who did not overwhelm his pupils with excessive work, and whose teaching, though uninteresting, was efficient, and, "despite the compulsion," not "distasteful." (p. 24) From Lamberciere he learnt Latin and the Calvinist catechism together "with all that sorry nonsense as well that goes by the name of education." (p. 23) Mlle. Lamberciere aroused his first erotic fantasies and desires. In 1724, after two happy years at Bossey, the cousins were recalled home by Bernard. A year later the young Jean-Jacques, aged nearly thirteen, was apprenticed with an engraver, a M. Ducommun, "an oafish and violent young man" who beat him savagely and frequently and "managed in a very short time to quench all the fire of my childhood, and to coarsen my affection and lively nature." (p. 39) One Sunday, the 14 March 1728, he returned late from a walking excursion outside the city and found the gates locked. This had happened twice before, each time it had earned himself a severe beating. This time, just short of his sixteenth birthday, he decided not to return to his master.

An aimless period of his life followed, of loitering about, lying and stealing, which he did as a sort of self-defence against his fate. Then we find him arriving, "restless and dissatisfied with myself," at the door of a Madame de Warens in Annecy. (p. 49) A devout twenty-nine years old Catholic convert, Warens, who was to have a decisive influence on his life, took him in providing he agreed to become a Catholic, a condition he accepted in his desperation, despite his "aversion to Catholicism," and his trepidation about losing his prized Genevan citizenship. (p. 67) Sent off to the Hospice of the Holy Spirit in Turin, Italy he was accepted into the Catholic faith on 21 April 1728. He left the Hospice with a bitter taste in his mouth, twenty francs in his pocket, and the exhortation to be a good Christian in his ear. For a short while he enjoyed his freedom, exploring the city, and "punctiliously" attending the royal mass at court where he heard "the best music in Europe." (p. 75) His funds exhausted, however, he was forced to seek employment as a liveried footman in the service of a Mme de. Vercellis.

These adolescent years were years of confusion; of adventure, romantic fantasies and sexual frustrations because of his shyness with women. His position in the Vercellis household was terminated when, stealing a colourful ribbon that belonged to the lady of the house and faced with detection, he tried to pin the robbery on an innocent serving girl. Both were dismissed, but the incident, trifling in itself, haunted him till the end of his life. At the time he took to visiting an Abbe Gaime, a young Savoyard priest whose acquaintance he had made at the Vercellis house. Gaime taught him "a sound morality" and "the principles of common sense," urged him to accept himself as he was, and encouraged him to believe that he could win his redemption by following Christ's ethical example. (p. 92) Gaime was, "to a great extent at least," his future model for the Savoyard Vicar in *Emile*, except that he expressed himself less frankly than the Vicar on "certain points." (p. 93)

Rousseau's next employment, with the de Gouvon family, brought him under the influence of the old Count's youngest son the Abbe, who engaged him as a secretary. His association with the Abbe rekindled his interest in learning and taught him Latin and Italian "in its purest form." From it he "acquired some taste for literature" and to discriminate between good and bad books. (p. 98) This promising employment, however, also came to a quick end through his fault following a needless quarrel with the Count over his new friendship with a young Genevan friend, a strange youth named M. Bacle. Aged nearly seventeen and jobless he drifted aimlessly with Bacle until their purse ran out. Then, in the Summer of 1729 he resolved to return to Warens who, despite his fear of an indifferent reception, welcomed him with open arms and promised her support and assistance. She became his *Maman* and he "fell into extravagances" of feeling over her, "that seemed as if they could only have been inspired by the most violent love." (p. 108) An M. d'Aubonne, a relative of *Maman*'s asked to assess his future prospects strangely declared that "… despite my promising appearance and lively features, he could not find an idea in my head or any trace of education." (p. 112) He was, at best, fitted for some small parish. So he was dispatched to a Lazarist seminary where he went "as if to the scaffold." (p. 116) The attempt to make him a priest failed, but one of his teachers, an M.Gatier, so impressed him with "his sensitiveness, and his affectionate, loving nature," that he became his second model for the Savoyard Vicar. (p. 118)

Encouraged by *Maman* Jean-Jacques's love for music grew, and he was next apprenticed with a Nicoloz Le Maitre a Parisian choirmaster, composer, and organist at the cathedral in Annecy. His apprenticeship, however, was brief and ended calamitously one night on the streets of Lyon when Le Maitre collapsed in a violent fit and the young man, panic-stricken, left him there to return home only to find that *Maman* had gone to Paris, no one knew where or for how long. He awaited her return patiently meanwhile trying his hand at musical composition, but when in late 1730 he had no news of her whereabouts, he was on the road to Fribourg accompanying a young servant of her household back to her family home. He returned to Geneva for the first time since he had left it four years earlier, and passed through Nyon where he resumed contact with his now re-married father and Lausanne where he passed himself off as a Parisian musician and music teacher. Even though *Maman* was never far from his thoughts, the prospect of employment as a companion to the nephew of a Swiss Colonel in the French service enticed him to Paris for the first time. His excitement with his visit was, however, replaced by deep shock when instead of the fine imposing city he had romanticised in his mind he found "dirty, stinking little streets, ugly black houses, a general air of squalor and poverty, beggars, carters, menders of clothes, sellers of herb-drinks, and old hats." This negative first impression of Paris was never to leave him and was eventually to turn into "a secret aversion to living in the capital." (p. 155)

Nothing came of the job, nor of his nearly frantic inquiries into *Maman*'s whereabouts. His financial problems were eased by a M. Rolichon who commissioned him to copy music, which he did poorly but proudly, later adopting it as his trade. Reunited finally with *Maman* at Chambery towards the end of 1731, she found him temporary work as a land surveyor. In 1733, alarmed by the "dangers of my youth," his exposure to the temptations of the flesh, she initiated him sexually, an experience which, though desired, brought him "mixed feelings of elation and a strange 'invincible sadness'." (p. 189) She was his *Maman* after all! It also distressed Claude Anet, her household administrator and covert lover, a "serious, even solemn," man of peasant origins and roughly her age, who later inspired the figure of Wolmar in *Heloise*. Anet was "undoubtedly a rare man, and the only one of his kind I have ever met. Slow, sedate, thoughtful, circumspect in his behaviour, cold in his manner, laconic and sententious in his conversation," though at times prone to hasty action, as an earlier suicide attempt over some petty disagreement with Warens showed. Rousseau speaks of becoming "in some sense his pupil," i.e. of adopting him as his mentor. (pp. 172–173) From him and *Maman* came his interest in botany which became a great passion in later years. *Maman* informed Anet of her new liaison and he endorsed it with some difficulty. "An alliance" was formed between the three which was "perhaps unique on earth," which "brought us all happiness, and which only death was strong enough to dissolve." (p. 173) In fact, Anet died soon after from pleurisy. But the idyllic *ménage a trois* created with him and *Maman* would be attempted with others later and would find its echo later in

Heloise, in *Emile*, and in Rousseau's political writing where it served as a model for the state also.

With Anet's death Rousseau became *Maman*'s new administrator. Without Anet's wise and firm guidance, however, she returned to an "old addiction for enterprises and schemes," that would eventually bring her to financial ruin. (p. 195) In 1736, moving with her into *Les Charmettes*, a suburban cottage just outside Chambery, Rousseau experienced "the short period of my life's happiness ... those peaceful but transient moments that have given me the right to say I have lived." (p. 215) Returning again briefly to Geneva in 1737 to finally reclaim his part of his mother's small inheritance, he visited his father and other relatives again, en route. Then a fateful acquaintance with a M. de Conzie, an erudite Savoyard gentleman friend of *Maman*'s, fired "the seeds of literature and philosophy" which "were beginning to stir in my brain," and led him to read Voltaire whose writing "fired me with the desire of learning to write a good style," and to imitate his "fine effects." (p. 205) However, he and *Maman* were drifting apart and he took increasingly to travelling on any pretext he could find. He also felt himself "drawn gradually towards study; meeting men of letters, listening to literary talk, and even sometimes daring to take part in it myself; but rather assuming a bookish jargon than gaining any real knowledge of a book's content." (p. 209) Now unhappy at home he also immersed himself in music and played chess. Then one day he suffered a sudden physical and mental collapse that was to cloud his whole life: "a kind of storm which started in my blood and instantly took control of my limbs." It left him with a permanent insomnia and "buzzings" in his head and prone to physical suffering and to periods of fatigue and dizziness for the rest of his life. (p. 217).

Maman nursed him to health and their intimacy returned. Convinced of his imminent death, he discussed religion at length with her. In the Winter of 1738 he "began to read, or rather to devour" the work of the seventeenth-century Port-Royal philosophers who "combined devotion and the sciences," with his doctor, an M. Salamon, "a great Cartesian," making him, in his own words, "half a Jansenist." (p. 221) By reading the Jansenists he became seriously disturbed by "the fear of hell which had bothered me very little before." (1770:1953: 230) However, his appetite for philosophy whetted we find him continuing avidly with his self-education, reading Locke, Malebranche, Leibnitz, Descartes and others, ambitious at first to reconcile their thinking into one system. But soon he wanted to go his own way and started to use them purely as "a store of ideas" for his "self-tuition," to create "a great enough fund of learning to be self-sufficient and to think without the help of another." (p. 226) This, thinking "without the help of another," became, as we shall see, his fundamental project in life and his educational ideal. Meanwhile he went for excursions into the countryside, worked the fields with the peasants, studied physiology and anatomy which, he tells us, fuelled his disposition to hypochondria, and, with improved health, took to travelling again. Then one day, returning from a longish trip, he had the shock of his life. *Maman* had formed a new attachment "a young man from the Vaud country" named Wintzenried. (p. 248) For Rousseau, it threw his "whole being," he says, "completely upside down." (p. 249) There was to be no *ménage a trois* with Wintzenried as there had been with Anet. He was no

Anet. So he had no other option but to leave, and Warens helped him find a job in Lyon as tutor to the two young sons of Jean Bonnot de Mably, grand provost of the city – his break with *Maman* was conclusive but his first engagement with education was about to begin.

2.–1749

His experience as a tutor with the Mably family was brief and unsuccessful. "I was not lacking in industry," he says, "but I had no patience and, worse still, no tact." The methods he used to control the boys, "the appeal to sentiment, argument, and anger," failed dismally. As any experienced teacher would have told him, they "are always useless and sometimes pernicious when employed on children." (p. 253) On the positive side, his connection with the Mably household gave him access to an educated and well-connected society well-versed in the current trends and issues fashionable in the cultured circles of Lyons and Paris, the world of the *philosophes* and of Enlightenment thinking. He met the Abbe de Mably and his brother the Abbe de Condillac, who were both to distinguish themselves later in the world of ideas. He wrote some poems and an opera and, more significantly for us, the *Project for the Education of M. de Sainte-Marie*, which was inspired by John Locke's seminal *Some Thoughts Concerning Education* of 1693. "Form in him the heart, the judgement, the mind, in that order," Rousseau advised the tutor, one's pupil is lost once one "has allowed his heart to be corrupted." Good sense has more to do with "the feeling of the heart than the brightness of the mind'." (Mason 1979, p. 20) These were precepts later passed on to Emile's tutor in *Emile*. The contribution of the arts and sciences to a young man's education advocated in the *Project*, however, "contradict(ed) his later rejection of 'civilization' in the *Discourses*." (Durant & Durant 1967, p. 14) Otherwise the pamphlet was unremarkable in itself, its message summarised in the valid but not very original argument that education is more than learning from books and should develop the judgement, sentiments, and spirit of the young man.

Resigning his employment with the Mably family in 1741 Rousseau returned to Paris "with fifteen *louis* in ready money, and with my comedy *Narcissus* and my scheme of notation my sole resources," but dreaming of success. (p. 266) In August of 1742, he was ready to present his original scheme of musical notation (with numerical instead of the standard arrangements), to the Academy of the Sciences in Paris. But, to his disappointment, it was tactfully turned down. In 1743 he re-wrote and published it as *A Dissertation on Modern Music*. (p. 268) That year he also began an opera in the French style, *The Gallant Muses*, and became friends with Denis Diderot, a year his junior who shared his social background and his interests in the arts and the sciences, and in social criticism. Diderot was later to commission him to write articles for the famous *Encyclopaedia*, the project on which he collaborated with Jean d'Alembert in 1748, and their friendship was to last for nearly fifteen years before coming to grief, like several others. In July 1743 Rousseau found employment as private secretary to the French ambassador in Venice the Comte de Montagiu. The ambassador, however, was a vain, miserly, and incompetent man, and they soon quarrelled, ostensibly over the payment of arrears in Rousseau's pay.

Within a year he was dismissed from his post and was back in Paris in August of 1744. In Venice he had acquired a greater knowledge of Italian and of Italian music which he had heard performed by the best ensembles in Europe. More importantly for us, he became interested in social theory and political institutions, and first conceived the idea of writing a political work on the subject which was later to become the *Social Contract.* "Everything," he had decided, "is rooted in politics" and "whatever might be attempted, no people would ever be other than the nature of their government made them," a conclusion which conditioned his later advocacy of public schooling. (p. 377) In 1745 he took Therese Levasseur, who worked as a laundress and seamstress in the cheap rooming house where he stayed, for his mistress. She was young, plain, and uneducated, but of a decent family. They were to live together for the next twenty-three years before he married her in 1768. With her he had five children, all of them dispatched at birth, at his insistence, to a foundling asylum – an act that became deeply embarrassing for the author of *Emile,* and which he felt constrained to defend until his dying days. Indeed, his remorse became so strong "that it almost drew from me a public confession of my fault at the beginning of *Emile.*" (p. 549) In 1761, he tried to re-trace them unsuccessfully and argued against the charge that he was "a man without feelings or compassion, an unnatural father," that his actions were motivated by the good of the children and his duty as a citizen, to prevent them from becoming "adventurers and fortune hunters." (p. 333) In the *Reveries* he insisted that "no man has ever loved seeing little children romping and playing together more than I do," (1776:1979, p. 139) and that the writing of *Heloise* and *Emile* was evidence that "I engaged in this study with the attentive care of someone who enjoyed his work." (p. 140)

His finished opera in 1745 failed to impress the foremost composer and musicologist in France at the time, Jean-Philippe Rameau, who listened to parts of it ungraciously and showed irritation throughout the performance, but it performed successfully at Court. Still, with his financial problems growing, he decided to give up on his musical ambitions and to devote "my time and energy to procuring a livelihood for myself and my dear Therese," by copying music. (p. 319) In 1746, however, his aristocratic connections brought him a lucrative post as secretary with the wealthy Dupin family at Chenonceaux in the Loire Valley. In the year following, 1747, his father died and he re-claimed that part of his mother's property which he had retrieved and which he had given to his father to enjoy while he had lived. Part of the money he sent to *Maman,* now in acute economic distress. His own finances improved considerably with his new employment and his circle of friends grew to include Condillac, d'Alembert, and Melchior Grimm. With the latter, in particular, he grew "firmly attached" because of their mutual interest in music. (p. 329) In 1748, he started work on the articles on music that Diderot commissioned for the *Encyclopaedia.* But Diderot himself was arrested that same year for writing the *Letter on the Blind* which endorsed Locke's empiricism and his theory of the mind as a *tabula rasa,* or blank slate. When his imprisonment was changed to house arrest in Vincennes, Rousseau, now thirty seven years old, took to visiting him regularly on foot. One fateful Summer day in 1749 on his way there he experienced a strange 'illumination' or vision, which he first described in his *Second Letter to*

M. de Malesherbes written in January 1762, then reported later in the *Confessions*, and which was to change his life radically.

The day was excessively hot, he tells us, the pruned trees on the wayside offered little or no shade. Exhausted by walking, he lay under a tree to regain his energies and took out of his pocket an edition of the *Mercure de France* to read. His eyes fell upon an item announcing a prize essay competition sponsored by the Academy of Dijon on the subject whether progress in the sciences and the arts has done more to corrupt morals or to improve them. "The moment I read this," he says, "I beheld another universe and became another man." (p. 327) The drama of the moment is vividly described in the *Letter*. His mind, he tells us, was "dazzled by a thousand lights," "crowds of lively ideas presented themselves at the same time," and he was seized by "a dizziness similar to drunkenness":

> "Oh Sir, if I had ever been able to write a quarter of what I saw and felt under that tree, how clearly I would have made all the contradictions of the social system seem, with what strength I would have exposed all the abuses of our institutions, with what simplicity I would have demonstrated that man is naturally good and that it is from these institutions alone that men become wicked. Everything that I was able to retain of these crowds of great truths which illuminated me under that tree in a quarter of an hour has been weakly scattered about in my three principal writings, namely that first discourse, the one about inequality, and the treatise on education, which three works are inseparable and together form the same whole." (Kelley et al. 1995, p. 575)

The "scales" fell from his eyes, the "chaos in his head" was "unscrambled," his excitement was uncontainable. Suddenly he saw "another universe, a true golden age, societies of simple, wise, happy men," to which he and his fellow men had grown blind. (1776a:1990, p. 131) Reaching Vincennes "in a state of agitation bordering on delirium" he told Diderot about the prize and read him a piece of writing he had jotted down some time earlier, named *Fabricius's Soliloquy*, which could be the first draft for his argument. Diderot applauded, and encouraged his project. "From that moment," he tells us, "I was lost." (1770:1953, p. 328)

CHAPTER 1

ON STATE EDUCATION

The Discourses and Poland

FIRST DISCOURSE: ATTACKING THE ENLIGHTENMENT

"Lost"! What did he mean? Rousseau competed for the Dijon prize with the *First Discourse*, on the sciences and the arts, which he wrote in the autumn of the same year 1749. Its controversial thesis and powerful rhetoric won him the prize. Published in 1750 it caught "like wildfire" in the cultural world of Paris, and he was an immediate celebrity. (1770:1953, p. 338) Views about him were radically divided from the start, however; "the moment my essay appeared," he remarks, "the champions of literature fell upon me as if on one accord." (p. 341) His views and his scathing attack on their integrity had antagonised the *philosophes*. Later he called it an "unhappy work" which was not received "as it deserved to be!" and that opened an avoidable "abyss of miseries" for him. ('Forward' to a 1781 edition, Cress 1987, p. xxii) But at the moment it was published his missionary zeal left him in no mood to compromise: "I have taken my stand," he declared, "I do not care about pleasing either the witty or the fashionable." (1750:1987, p. 1)

Oddly Diderot had approved of its draft version and, it would seem, undertook to print it also in the *Encyclopaedia*. 'Oddly' because the *Discourse* was written to challenge projects like the *Encyclopaedia*, which emblemized the Enlightenment's celebration of the sciences and the arts as marks of the civilized progress of contemporary society, in a most radical way, representing them instead as sources and symptoms of social degeneration. Rousseau opens it (prophetically as it turned out) by installing himself, like the heroic Socrates of the *Apology*, in the political role of society's gadfly, seeking not fame and honour, like the *philosophes*, but only the reward Socrates finally achieved for himself; the survival of his reputation for virtue throughout the ages. Contemporary society he declared a society of slaves, of men who had lost the "original liberty" that was theirs by birthright. Far from contributing to their freedom the sciences and the arts had "spread garlands of flowers over the iron chains" that shackle them, (p. 3) lent governments the tools with which to crush them into "a vile and deceitful uniformity," and taught them to love their slavery. (p. 4) "Our souls," he declared, "have become corrupted in proportion as our sciences and our arts have advanced towards perfection." (p. 5) Hence, like his mentor Socrates, he advocated banning 'poetry' from the city and praised the hard, practical minded Romans, his heroes together with the Spartans, as a people who were "dazzled neither by vain pomp nor by studied elegance." (p. 10)

Society, he said, needed wise, fearless, men like Socrates willing to bear witness to the value of 'ignorance' and simplicity, men who recognise the limitations that

1

nature imposes on human knowledge for our own good, and are respectful of the ultimate secrets it conceals from us. The implication is clear; he would be such a man for his society. Aspiring to possess these secrets is arrogant, even blasphemous (since it presumes the ability to read the mind of the Creator), and a waste of time and energy, since pursuing them does not conduce to virtue or better morals. To the contrary it produces a materialist mentality that distorts and exploits what is natural. Rousseau accused the *philosophes* of *amour-propre*, a hunger for praise and honours that gives rise to vain narcissism, and dismissed them as "a troop of charlatans each crying from his own place on a public square." (p. 18) He charged them with caring nothing for truth, and adjusting their genius to their thirst for popularity. *Amour-propre*, he affirmed, is the sentiment that undermines society, brings about the dissolution of public mores and corrupts virtue and taste among men and women. Contemporary education, which should serve the interests of moral and civic progress, is "foolish," and its institutions serve only to "corrupt our judgment":

> "Everywhere I see immense establishments where youths are brought up at great expense to learn everything but their duties. Your children will not know their own language, but will speak others which are nowhere in use. They will know how to compose verses they will scarcely be capable of comprehending. Without knowing how to separate error from truth, they will possess the art of making themselves unrecognizable to others by means of specious arguments. But they will not know the meaning of the words magnanimity, fair-mindedness, temperance, humanity, courage. The sweet name homeland will never strike their ear; and if they hear God spoken of at all, it will be less to be in awe of him than to be in fear of him." (p. 16)

"We have physicists, geometers, chemists, astronomers, poets, musicians, painters," but "we no longer have citizens." (p. 17) He repeats his view from the *Project* that children must be kept occupied at all times since idleness brings loss of innocence. What they should be learning is a "fine question" he was not yet ready to address – it would wait for *Emile*. But the passage quoted supplies an early indication of how he perceived the proper ingredients of education. Children must learn: (i) their duties and be socialised into their native, home-spun, culture; (ii) to value honest and forthright debate and the mind set that goes with it; (iii) the virtues of magnanimity, fair-mindedness, temperance, humanity, and courage; (iv) patriotic zeal, and; (v) awe towards their Creator. These are the ingredients of the public education he would describe later, in his *Third Discourse* and in *Poland* – they would also be the qualities possessed by Emile. For now he was occupied with a critique of his society that was entirely destructive. The institutions of state censorship that should guard the public from corrupt ideas and visions were well-intentioned but ineffective, the invention of printing a disaster that had permitted the circulation of "the dangerous reveries of the likes of Hobbes and Spinoza." (p. 19) The *Discourse* finishes with an exhortation to God that must have read doubly provocative to the 'atheist' *philosophes*: "to deliver us "from the enlightenment and the deadly arts of our fathers, and give back to us ignorance, innocence and poverty – the only goods that can bring about our happiness and that are precious in your sights." (p. 19)

Many years later he protested that he had never been "able to discover the cause of this extraordinary turn of events" that had turned the *philosophes*, his erstwhile friends, into his enemies but it was he who threw his gauntlet down and provoked their anger. (1776b:1979, p. 126) The suggestion in the *Dialogues* is that he perceived them as "ardent missionaries" of atheism and materialism with which, he claimed, they had influenced "the institutions of men," and which conflicted with the "lofty ideas I had of the divinity." (1776a:1990, pp. 52–53) He was convinced that their philosophy "does nothing but destroy," hence his declaration of war. (p. 53) They replied by charging him with duplicity; "while he disparages the arts," they said, "he himself writes plays, music and operas." (Dent 2005, p. 56) His friend Grimm described the *Discourse*'s thesis as a plea for a 'return to nature', and as "devilish nonsense," and mischievously asked the question that bedevils all 'state of nature' theories – "What is 'nature'?" (Durant & Durant 1967, p. 23)

Rousseau himself later admitted to the *Discourse*'s shortcomings, describing it as "the most feebly argued," of his work and "completely lacking in logic and order," but he defended himself vigorously against its critics at the time, and put his defence together in his 1753 'Preface' to his play *Narcissus*. (Simpson 2007, p. 34) Grimm's question he addressed fully not long after in his *Second Discourse*. Meanwhile, he changed his life-style to accord with the ideals of modesty and plainness promoted in the *First Discourse*. He explicitly acknowledges the Jansenist influence on his conversion, of being "constantly in fear of error," of endangering his soul for the sake of earthly pleasures. (1776b:1979, p. 54) He sought, he tells us, to put his life in order and to secure "an assured role of conduct for the rest of my days." (p. 53) And it was this "change in my character," rather than his newly-found literary celebrity, he believed, that really provoked the hostility of the *philosophes*. "They would perhaps have forgiven me for brilliance in the art of writing," he reflects, "but they could not forgive me for setting up an example by my conduct; this appeared to put them out." (1770:1953, p. 338) However, at the age of forty and in "the fullness of my mental powers" at the time, he was in no mood for compromise. (1776b:1979, p. 53) "Gold lace and white stockings," were abandoned and he "wore a round wig." (1770:1953, p. 339) He gave up his sword, sold his watch, and prepared himself to launch into "what were perhaps the most ardent and sincere investigations ever conducted by any mortal." (1776b:1979, p. 54) This was to be his new mission.

BREAKING WITH FRIENDS: (1750–1758)

Consistently with his new philosophy of life he resigned his lucrative Dupin employment and turned to copying music again to earn his living. This, as I remarked earlier, he continued to regard as his trade for life; 'literature', despite that it occupied most of his time, was a "distraction … prejudicial to my daily employment." (1770:1953, p. 341) "Writing books to make a living," he was to explain years later, "would have made me dependent on the public." (1776a:1990) His "only thought" now, he says, was to make the reforms to his life "solid and lasting by striving to uproot from my heart all tendencies to be affected by the judgment of men," i.e. all tendencies to *amour-propre*, that could deflect him, "out of fear of reproach, from conduct that was good and reasonable in itself." (1770:1953, p. 340) What he promised his fellows was pure honesty; there was to be no "twisting his morality to his own benefit," no room for *amour-propre* in his life. (1776a:1990, p. 175) These would be the qualities into which Emile would also be educated. A "strict self-examination" was required to "order my inner life for the rest of my days as I would wish it to be at the time of my death" – the self-examination or 'profession' of the Vicar. (1776b:1979, p. 51) His "intellectual world" he now governed with "a simple and dignified economy," his tone became "sharp and biting," his "contempt" for bourgeois society open. (1770:1953, p. 388) "Deluded by my stupid conceit," as he was to describe it later, he believed that he could change it. (p. 387) He was so transformed, he says, that "my friends and acquaintances no longer recognised me," a foreigner in their midst, as Emile's education would make Emile. (p. 388) Meanwhile, his domestic life was not going well; with the "wrangling and the daily disagreeableness" created by Therese's family, her mother in particular, he "plunged" himself "entirely into literature as a way of escape," and this was, he says, his fatal error. (p. 343)

In 1752, he involved himself in a politically charged polemic over the respective merits of French and Italian music, in other words of Rameau and Pergolesi, controversially taking the Italian side. An opera he wrote in the Italian style with French lyrics, *The Village Soothsayer*, was successfully performed before the king at Fontainebleu, became a financial success, and "brought me completely into fashion," so that "no man in Paris was more sought after than I." (p. 344) A successful performance of *Narcissus* by the *Comedie Francaise* followed in December of that year. But his *Letter on French Music* (1753), a frontal attack on Rameau's *Treatise on Harmony*, published the year after, "raised the whole nation against me" and he was hung in effigy in the streets of Paris; a fore-taste of what was to come years later for a different reason. (p. 358) In November of 1753 the Dijon Academy announced another prize-essay. The subject, 'What is the origin of inequality among men, and is it justified by natural law?' suited him perfectly. He submitted his answer to the question with the *Second Discourse* in 1754 but, though he regarded it as "a work of the greatest importance," the *Discourse* failed to win him the prize this time. (p. 361)

In June of 1754 he returned to Geneva. On his way there he saw *Maman*, for the last time as it turned out. The experience disturbed him deeply: "In what a state, Oh God! How low she had fallen! What was left to her of her former virtue?" (p. 364) On the other hand he was "feted and made much of by all classes" of citizens in Geneva to whom he had dedicated the *Second Discourse*. His "republican enthusiasm" aroused by this reception he returned publicly to the Calvinist faith and reclaimed his citizenship. (p. 365) But the *Discourse* itself was coldly received in the city and Voltaire's (now his arch rival) decision to live close by, decided him against settling there. He was back in Paris within four months, only to leave it again in April 1756 for a small but charming and secluded residence close to Montmorency named the 'Hermitage', placed at his disposal by a wealthy friend, Mme. D'Epinay.

There, away from controversy and the publicity of city life, he resumed his solitary walks and worked on the book on *Political Institutions* he had first conceived thirteen years earlier in Venice, and compiled extracts from the Abbe de Saint-Pierre's *Project for Perpetual Peace* for later publication in 1761. In July/August of 1756 he entered another controversy, this time with Voltaire himself, provoked by his *Letter to Voltaire on Providence* which criticised Voltaire's views on the workings of divine providence and its influence on the world, expressed in two didactic poems. The *Letter* drew Voltaire's response later in his famous parable *Candide* (1759). That same year Rousseau worked on his *Essay on the Origin of Languages* which was never finished, and on another book, *The Morals of Sensibility or The Wise Man's Materialism*, which had the same fate. In autumn he began to write *Heloise* and was already planning *Emile*. In 1757 a painful and embarrassing infatuation with a much younger woman than himself, Sophie d'Houdetot, which again aroused his dream of a *manage a trois* with her lover, an M. de Saint-Lambert, produced the *Moral Letters*. Sophie, who "was not in the least beautiful," but attractive nonetheless, inspired the character of Julie in *Heloise*. (p. 409) Meanwhile, his deteriorating relations with Diderot and Grimm, both of whom he believed to be in league with his enemies in the 'Holbach circle', and a painful quarrel with Mme. d'Epinay led him to leave the 'Hermitage' for a new home in Mont-louis. In September of that year, 1757, he published his *Letter to M. d'Alembert on the Theatre* in reply to an earlier article d'Alembert had published in Volume VII of the *Encylopaedia* which had complimented the city of Geneva on various things but criticised the fact that it banned the theatre which, he had argued, is important for educating the taste of citizens. The article had caused uproar and indignation in the city and Rousseau's *Letter* took the Genevan side in the matter, opposing the idea of a Genevan theatre with moral, social and aesthetic arguments. A great financial success it brought him the added satisfaction that d'Alembert, who he believed to be also in league with the 'circle' which, he thought, persecuted him, was forced to resign as co-editor of the *Encyclopaedia* with Diderot. His conclusive break with Diderot himself and with Grimm followed soon after in 1758.

SECOND DISCOURSE: SELF-SUFFICIENT MAN

The appeal to nature was not by any means original to Rousseau's thought, it was already central to Enlightenment thinking, and had long been a subject of controversy, when the *First Discourse* appeared. A century earlier, the English materialist philosopher Thomas Hobbes had represented human nature as naturally vicious, aggressive, and acquisitive in his famous book *The Leviathan* (1651). Hobbes had described the 'state of nature', of absolute freedom from law or moral restriction, as one of unrelenting war of each against each, where life is 'short nasty and brutish', and where civilized existence is impossible. In these circumstances Hobbes represented 'men's' transition into civil society through a compact made between themselves individually, and collectively with a ruler, as a net gain notwithstanding that it required them to alienate their individual freedom to an all-powerful sovereign who would guarantee their protection in return. In the *First Discourse* Rousseau had already dismissed this theory as a "dangerous reverie". In the *Second*, while he agreed with Hobbes that the basic human instinct is of self-preservation and well-being, and called it *amour de soi*, he described an original state very different from Hobbes's, where men were happy and at peace with themselves and others in their self-sufficiency.

Rousseau was right to describe the *Second Discourse*, written under the proud *nom de plume* 'Citizen of Geneva', a superior work to the *First*. Its content is undoubtedly more scholarly and in between the writing of the two *Discourses* he had steeped himself in the French moralizing tradition headed by Montaigne and Montesquieu bringing a new sophistication to the work. Also, though its thesis is "even more radical," than that of the *First Discourse* it is "less ridden by paradox and more complex," as a work. (Gay 1987, p. 25) The 'Letter' of dedication in the preface addressed to the Lords and citizens of the Genevan Republic is an important political statement in its right, his first sketch of an ideal state which would be fleshed out years later in the *Social Contract*. His ideal, the state he would choose to live in, he says in the 'Letter', would be so intimate that "neither the obscure manoeuvres of vice nor the modest of virtue could be hidden from the notice and the judgement of the public," (1755a:1987, p. 26) a state which would serve a small tight community of citizens, where "it is easy for the people to gather together" and where each citizen can easily know all the others, (1762a:1987, p. 180) founded on healthy families where the men are active citizens in the public sphere and the women perform their ideal role of "chaste guardians of mores and the gentle bonds of peace," i.e. of keeping their families morally intact and healthy, (p. 32) where love of homeland (the absence of which in European societies he had lamented in the *First Discourse*) is "love of the citizens" rather than "of the land," i.e. where patriotism is based on a generalised sentiment of fraternity rather than on an abstract nationalism, (p. 26) where the citizens enjoy the protection of secure borders and are not threatened by any expansionist ambitions by the state, and, more critically, where strong and tried democratic institutions render them sovereign. His 'Letter' claimed that these were conditions already found in the city-state of Geneva.

The *Discourse* proper is opened with the claim that the study of 'man' is the most crucial but least advanced branch of human knowledge; necessary for an understanding of the political sources of the inequality and betrayal of freedom he had described in the *First Discourse*. The central question the *Second Discourse* addresses is how did the strong "resolve to serve the weak, and the people to buy imaginary repose at the price of felicity?" (p. 38) The investigation prepares the way for the *Third Discourse* which is about political institutions, about "the fundamental compact of all government" *per se*, which would, in turn, be necessary to prepare the ground for the *Social Contract*, (p. 75) which "takes men as they are," as nature made them, and describes the "laws as they might be" in an ideal, or well-ordered, state. (1762a:1987, p. 141) Rousseau promises a study of 'man' free from "metaphysical subtleties" or supernatural explanations, and which would lay claim to no "historical truths." (1755a:1987, p. 34) Its findings would be "hypothetical and conditional … better suited to shedding light on the nature of things than to pointing out their true origin." (pp. 38–39) Written as an anthropological/historical/social narrative it begins from the beginning, with 'natural man' (Rousseau uses the term for members of the male sex, not as a generic term for human beings in general) in his first, pre-social, state – "a creature scarcely recognisable in contemporary man" (p. 33), and continues with a stage by stage description of his evolution into the contemporary bourgeois man whose condition was described in the *First Discourse*.

Modern anthropology tells us that Rousseau's natural man never existed, but he recognised as much himself, referring to his writing as "hypothetical history." (Reisert 2003, p. 35) He describes his natural man as a self-sufficient, solitary, primitive being "satisfying his hunger under an oak tree, quenching his thirst at the first stream, finding his bed at the foot of the same tree that supplied his meal," satisfying his sexual urges randomly, happy because "all his needs are satisfied." (p. 40) This self-sufficiency, of having no more than one needs and needing no more than what lies within one's power to have is also, for Rousseau, the standard of human happiness. Apart from *amour de soi*, his self-love, natural man's other basic sentiment is 'pity' which he experiences in the presence of the pain and suffering of other sentient beings, humans more particularly, and which induces the first social urge in him. (p. 35) So deeply embedded in human nature is this sentiment that even "the most depraved mores still have difficulty destroying it." (p. 54) What activates it is a "kind of instinct in pressing circumstances, to beg for help in great dangers, or for relief of violent ills" which, in turn, occasions the need to communicate with others and marks the beginning of human language. (p. 49).

From the two natural sentiments of *amour de soi* and pity, Rousseau says, flow all the rules of natural right. "The state of reflection," he continues, provocatively in an age that announced itself as the age of Reason, is "contrary to nature," corrupted by *amour-propre* it creates "a depraved animal." (p. 42) This 'depraved animal' is the 'slave' already identified in the *First Discourse*; namely bourgeois man. Natural man, to the contrary, is robust, agile and hardy, his lifestyle simple and regular, of vigorous spirit and with an intelligent instinct for survival, not vulnerable to illness, disease and the fear of death. What distinguishes him from other animals and renders his soul "spiritual," or truly free, is not his reason but his power of agency, his ability to choose his fate. (p. 45) Living for the day he is drawn neither to speculation nor to foresight; "The only goods he knows in the universe are nourishment, a woman, and rest; the only evils he fears are pain and hunger." Philosophy is unnatural for him but he possesses an "almost unlimited ... faculty of self-perfection," which Rousseau refers to as 'perfectibility' and which drives him to seek his continuous self-improvement in relation to nature and to his fellows. (p. 46)

Rousseau always regarded the first permanent human association, the nuclear family, as the natural and, therefore, the ideal social unit, visualising it as a co-operative whole embodying the happy self-sufficiency of the solitary individual at the social level. The nuclear family evolves in his narrative into the extended family first then into neighbourly associations and more complex settlements, then into civil society. The original self-sufficiency of the nuclear family is progressively eroded in the process, eventually requiring the regulation of laws and civil institutions. Festivals were what brought people together at first and they remained Rousseau's favoured mode of conviviality or social sharing. But the abundant leisure time which grew with security, and prosperity, and a settled existence, led to the creation of luxuries and different kinds of possessions or ownership on which people learnt to grow more and more dependent for their happiness. Merit, beauty, opulence became desirable and desired qualities.

Thus the seeds of *amour-propre*, of living in the approval of others, were planted in the human soul which came to be corrupted with the artificial and negative sentiments of vanity, envy, shame, contempt, and outraged pride; and with them the thirst for revenge and retribution. Evolving social mores fixed sexual desire "exclusively on one single object," creating the "artificial sentiment" of fidelity, which women, he says, extol mainly "to establish their hegemony and make dominant the sex that ought to obey;" a classical case of the strong serving the weak. (p. 56) The sentiment of fidelity is grounded in the self-same motive which inspires men to possess property; the institution that eventually gives rise to the creation of a civil society. In the institution of property Rousseau finds the origin of the social inequality that "wreaks so much havoc among us." (p. 56) "The first person who, having enclosed a plot of land, took it into his head to say this is mine, and found people simple enough to believe him," he declares in a famous statement later echoed in the literature of anarchism and revolutionary socialism alike, "was the true founder of civil society." (p. 60) With it inequality and slavery were institutionalised into the state – the question of the *Second Discourse* was answered.

The supplementary institution of inheritance then radicalized the division of society into the wealthy and the dispossessed, the master and the servant which, in any case, Rousseau tells us, is illusory, for there are no real masters and servants, all are 'slaves' in their dependence each on the other. Hence, his famous opening declaration in the *Social Contract* later that "Man is born free, and everywhere he is in chains," and that he "who believes himself the master of others, does not escape being more of a slave than they." (1762a:1987, p. 141) His judgment of the contemporary society that evolved from this condition in the *Second Discourse* is as stark and uncompromising as in the *First*: "The usurpation of the rich, the acts of brigandage of the poor, the unbridled passions of all," he says, "stifles natural pity and the still weak voice of justice," and men are universally "greedy, ambitious and wicked." (1755a:1987, p. 68) The tables are turned on Hobbes. The depraved condition Hobbes described as the state of nature is the state of the 'advanced' civil society in Rousseau's narrative. The social compact that Hobbes lauds for civilising civil society, in Rousseau's eyes, only:

> "gave new fetters to the weak and new forces to the rich, irretrievably destroyed natural liberty, established forever the law of property and of inequality, changed adroit usurpation into irrevocable right, and for the profit of a few ambitious men henceforth subjected the entire human race to labour, servitude, and misery." (p. 70)

Re-defining it by returning to the model of nature would be the business of the *Social Contract*. But there was more work to be done first in the *Third Discourse*.

THE POLITICS OF THE CONTRACT

There is a popular misconception about Rousseau that he advocated a 'return to nature', to the idyllic condition of the savage as his response to the disordered society of the day. In the *Social Contract*, however, he makes it clear that he saw man's transition from a pre-social to a social state as a net gain rather than as a loss for humanity, for as a result his:

> "faculties are exercised and developed, his ideas are broadened, his feelings are ennobled, his entire soul is elevated to such a height that, if the abuse of this condition did not often lower his status to beneath the level he left, he ought constantly to bless the happy moment that pulled him away from it forever and which transformed him from a stupid, limited animal into an intelligent being and a man." (1762a:1987, p. 151)

It is this "abuse of this condition" that the *Social Contract* wants to rectify. The social contract, or compact, is the means with which men create civil society, a good in itself it "substitutes a moral and legitimate equality," based on convention and right, for the natural inequality of "force and intelligence," that characterises the primitive, pre-social, state. (p. 153) It guarantees men a certainty of possession based on legal title not force, and substitutes a "moral liberty" based on an intelligent *will* "which alone can make man truly master of himself," for the liberty of dumb inclination that constitutes his absolute freedom in his pre-social state. (p. 151) One may ask whether this is not conceding to Hobbes. Not really, because Rousseau believed that to find the key to the salvation of the contemporary society requires returning to nature for clues to re-create man and re-devise society as it would be, an association of free equals, had not the lure of property and *amour-propre* deviated it from its course. This would be the political task of the *Social Contract*. His confidence that this could happen was based on his optimistic belief that nature's imprint on humanity is indestructible: "It is … the life of your species that I am about to describe to you according to the qualities you have received, which your education and your habits have been able to corrupt but have been unable to destroy," he says in the *Third Discourse*. (1755b:1987, p. 39)

In the *Social Contract* as in the *Third Discourse*, and in Part 2 of the *Second Discourse*, Rousseau argues that legitimacy is conferred on the state not by right of conquest nor by a people's fear of anarchy but by their anxiety "to defend their liberty." Hence, sovereignty always remains theirs. (1755a:1987, p. 72) Men cannot, as Hobbes had held, legitimately alienate their freedom or sell themselves as slaves, because such behaviour amounts to the renunciation of "one's dignity as a man, the rights of humanity and even its duties" for which there "is no possible compensation." (1762a:1987, p. 144) In the *Second Discourse* he had already argued that a true, or legitimate, compact is "between the populace and the leaders it chooses for itself," not one that is imposed on it by force. Once made the populace "has united all its wills into a single one," which, he says, is "the essence of the state" and which expresses itself in its laws. (1755a:1987, p. 75) This same line of thinking is pursued in the *Third Discourse* and the *Social Contract* where he refers to this "single will" as a 'general will'; i.e. a will that unites all wills into one. Only unconditional adherence to this united will of the people, this general will, he insists in all three works, guarantees genuine social order and true equality. Its authority, unlike paternal authority which endures only for as long as nature renders the child dependent on the father (after which the father is owed "merely respect and not obedience"), is never outgrown because it draws its power not from nature but from civil society itself; from the compact on which it is founded. (p. 74)

This distinction between domestic and state economy first made in the *Second Discourse* is pursued in depth in the *Third Discourse* where, defining the word 'economy' according to its Greek meaning as "wise and legitimate government" he warns against confusing the two together. (1755b:1987, p. 111) Yet, in the *Social Contract* he refers to the family as "the prototype of political societies," a significant change, where what he has in mind is a patriarchal family. "The leader," he says, "is the image of the father, the populace is the image of the children ... none give up their liberty except for their utility." The "entire difference" is that children love their father to repay him for the care he takes of them," but in the case of the leader "the pleasure of commanding takes the place of this feeling" – which implies an impersonal relationship between the leader and his people. (1762a:1987, p. 142) In the *Third Discourse* Rousseau calls the economy used "in relation to the government of persons" education, (1755b:1987, p. 127) and he retains the same definition of education as government in *Emile* (1762b:1991, p. 33), although, paradoxically, *Emile*, as we shall see, seems to offer itself to the reader, and has been read over the years by educators, as a pedagogy of freedom *from* government. It is not surprising, given this definition of education as "the government of persons," that in both the *Third Discourse* and in the *Social Contract* he characterizes the state as educator, but in the two cases the state, as we shall see, educates differently. In the *Third Discourse* it needs institutions of public instruction, or schools as we call them.

His thoughts on these institutions will be the subject of the next section. Meanwhile, in the *Third Discourse* Rousseau takes up the analogy Plato made in *The Republic* between the body politic and the body of the human individual which leads him, like Plato, to assume that the government (and hence the education) of the two is essentially similar: "The life of both is the *self* common to the whole, the reciprocal sensibility and the internal coordination of all the parts." (1755b:1987, p. 114, italics in original) This "coordination of the parts" is what Rousseau understood by 'order', which is also, like Plato, how he regarded justice. Without it the 'self' (whether of the individual man or the collective) is disordered and forfeits its identity and stability. The man dies morally by losing his virtue, the collective degenerates into anarchy and injustice. Both individual and collective self are moral beings with a will; the collective will is expressed as the general will. Its laws are supreme over every individual will; like "the voice of God," their pronouncement renders them absolute and infallible. (p. 115) In *Emile* Rousseau identifies moral conscience as the voice of God speaking to the individual from within. Both the political law of the collective and the law of conscience are corrupted by vice which ultimately stems from *amour-propre*, creating the disordered state and the disordered man respectively.

Being absolute and infallible the pronouncements of the general will are, like those of conscience, uncompromising; they demand "the total alienation of each associate, together with all of his rights, to the entire community." (1762a:1987, p. 148) The crucial question the *Social Contract* asks, the most "formidable difficulty" for the theory of legitimate government, as he referred to it in the *Third Discourse*, is how this 'alienation' of individual freedom which, as for Hobbes, must be absolute, can square with autonomy; in short, how men can be *both* free and under their own laws *and* subject to the collective will. (1755b:1987, p. 116) His famous and ingenious solution follows this line of reasoning: (1) "since each person gives himself whole and entire [to the general will], the condition is equal for everyone"; (2) "since the condition is equal for everyone, no one has an interest in making it burdensome for the others"; (3) "since the alienation is made without reservation, the union is as perfect as possible, and no associate has anything further to demand"; and, finally (4) "in giving himself to all, each person gives himself to no one." (1762a:1987, p. 148) Rousseau does not assume that the laws and edicts of the general will, will always be true, but that they will "always tends toward the public utility," in an ordered state. (p. 155) His answer to the possibility of the prospective dissident is that he will "merely [be] forced to be free." (p. 150) The "merely" has raised more than a few eyebrows with his modern critics who perceive this notion of a forced freedom as a dangerous paradox. But Rousseau did not think like his critics, he conceived of freedom differently, not as an affirmation of one's individuality but as freedom to do one's duty by obeying the law whether of one's conscience in the realm of private morality as a man, or the edicts of the general will in the public realm as a citizen.

Amelie Oksenberg Rorty, summarizing Rousseau's point "that in a just polity, the individual has only alienated his powers to himself under another name," describes it as little more than a clever piece of intellectual legerdemain. (1996, p. 245) She points out that the kind of political contract described in the *Social Contract* requires "a New Man with a new psychology," and criticises Rousseau for not showing how this could be achieved. (p. 245) But the answer is in the education of Emile which is designed precisely to create such a man. She also, like many another commentator before and after her, finds the figure of a 'Legislator' which Rousseau introduces into the *Social Contract*, paradoxical in a political theory which would seem to gravitate around the sovereignty of the general will. Dent calls it "perplexing." (2005, p. 140) But the Legislator, as will be pointed out further down, plays a critical part in Rousseau's general educational/political economy; it is replicated in *Heloise* in the figure of the Paterfamilias and in *Emile* in that of the Tutor; both, in turn, idealizations of Rousseau himself who aspired to the role. (Reisert 2003, p. x)

Meanwhile, Rousseau tempers this absolutist tendency of the general will by emphasising that it's authority applies only to those aspects of the individual's life and practices of freedom that concern the common good and the condition of equality; it cannot impose on him "fetters that are of no use to the community." (1762a:1987, p. 157) In such cases "every man can completely dispose of such goods and freedom as has been left to him." (p. 158) In short, while he limits the jurisdiction of the collective authority to the *res publica*, to the public business, he creates a realm of private freedom which belongs to the 'man' as distinct from the citizen, which the collective cannot legitimately legislate into obedience, and which is subject entirely to the laws of one's conscience. This distinction between public and private, between the citizen and the man was influential on modern liberal democratic politics later. It enabled him to reconcile his unorthodox private religious beliefs described in the *Profession* with his orthodox religious practice as a Calvinist or Catholic citizen.

On the other hand he dismissed the idea that the politics of the general will should be modelled on the direct Athenian democracy where the people's sovereignty was expressed in a system of constant plebiscite, and warned that the general will must not be confused with the will of a voting majority either, or even with the votes of all counted together. Like Plato he is critical of the unreliability of the democratic voice, of the incompetence of the democratic voter, and of the inherently confrontational and divisive nature of democratic politics in general. A wise collective vision is unitary not fragmented, its laws make towards the common good not towards factional or party interests, but it is difficult for a democratic government to unite the things it supposes itself to unite; an intimate society, simplicity of mores, equality in ranks and fortune, and the possession of little or no luxury. (p. 180) These are qualities that are beyond the grasp of ordinary citizen or collective notwithstanding that they may want and seek them. A *deus ex machina*, an external agent is required for that purpose; the third, patriarchal, figure in the political *manage a trois*, with the government (his wife) and the people (his children). This is the wise Legislator (who was usually in ancient times also the founder of the state, like Lycurgus for instance) who Rousseau brings into the picture to give the state its constitution as the embodiment of the social contract. No popular ratification for the laws is required when they are made if they are consistent with the constitution; their silent obedience signifies the people's consent to them, their tacit approval.

The Legislator is to the general will what God is to the individual conscience, the Father to the household, the Tutor to Emile, ever-present but invisible: "The engineer who invents the machine" of the state while the prince or government "constructs it and makes it run." (p. 163) A wise and unique genius, he is an acute and sensitive but, at the same time, a dispassionate observer of humanity, of his people. His reason is not coloured by his feelings and is beyond the comprehension of the populace, just as God's is beyond that of ordinary mortals. His authority is not coercive but persuasive, not actually written or pronounced in any edict, but handed down; not the authority of a magistrate or sovereign which expresses some sort of coercion, but the charismatic authority of a "great soul," (p. 165) "which can compel without violence and persuade without convincing," (p. 164) like Moses whom God gifted with the just eloquence to move his people into obedience. (Johnston 1999, p. 54) Like any wise engineer/ "architect," he "surveys and tests the ground" first, "to see if it can bear the weight." Like a wise Father or Tutor he "does not begin by laying down laws that are good in themselves," he sees that "the people for whom they are destined are fitted to bear them," first. (p. 165) His happiness, as we saw, comes not from popular acclaim but from "the pleasure of commanding," from the respect and obedience he receives from the people as their master. This is exactly, as we shall see, the same description Rousseau makes of the Tutor in *Emile* and the Father in *Heloise* – all in fact educate through their government. Oksenberg Rorty describes the educational strategies that follow the will of this "benign, paternalistic, unflawed Legislator-Tutor," as deeply problematic, but this issue will be returned to later, in the last chapter of this book. (1996, p. 244)

ON PUBLIC INSTRUCTION

"It is certain that in the long run people are what their government makes them," Rousseau says in making his case for public or state instruction in the *Third Discourse* – echoing a conclusion made many years before in Venice. "Train men if you want to command them," is a fundamental principle of government. The necessity to provide special institutions for this purpose he describes as "one of the fundamental maxims of popular or legitimate government," and the state's most urgent business. They must not, however, train men into blind obedience of the laws: "If you want the laws obeyed," he warns, "make them beloved;" i.e. make the citizens make them their own. (1755b:1987, p. 119) This precept holds equally for the Tutor in the education of the man, and the Father in the education of his household. Rousseau's statement in the *Social Contract* that "Every individual can, as a man, have a private will contrary to or different from *the general will that he has* as a citizen," (1762a:1987, p. 150 italics added) denotes that education into obedience of the general will be such that every citizen will make the general will his own, internalize it personally so that it "penetrates to the inner part of a man," and is "exerted no less on his will than on his actions." (1755b:1987, p. 119) Hence, to act in accord with the general will mean for each citizen, "to act in accordance with the maxim of his own judgement and not to be at odds with himself," the perfect object of education whether of the man or the citizen. (p. 117) As a citizen "his private will is in conformity with the general will in all things, and we willingly want what is wanted by the people we love," i.e. in the intimate community of the ideal state of the *Social Contract*, all one's fellow citizens. (p. 121) This sense of not being at odds with oneself and one's fellow-citizens is the closest to the original self-sufficiency in the state of nature men can achieve as social beings. It constitutes the moral and political definition of being 'a man' and a citizen respectively. Cultivating it will be the aim of Emile's education, achieving it the mark of his true freedom. The authority of the general will, like the authority of the Father and the Tutor, must, on its part, be exercised with wisdom rather than severity. Indeed, the key to all good government/education, Rousseau insists repeatedly in all his works, is not to punish crime or misdemeanour severely when it occurs but to prevent it from occurring. This is the politics of 'negative education', the same adopted by his tutor in Emile's education.

The object of public schools in the *Third Discourse* is to create citizens who will internalize the collective will expressed by the laws of the state. The curriculum and regulations are "prescribed by the government" and placed under the jurisdiction of "the magistrates put in place by the sovereign," (p. 125) a principle taken from Sparta "where the law kept watch chiefly over the education of children." (1755a:1987, p. 77) The curriculum's political agenda will be to cultivate love of the laws and of the homeland, a patriotic citizenry where patriotism is identified with love for the state – the political 'self'. Patriotism is the social and political glue that holds the collective together, a condition indispensable for the existence and exercise of a general will and citizen solidarity. The citizens' love for the state is reciprocated on the state's part by the assiduous care it takes for their welfare. This is the political perspective the young are taught at school in their education as citizens. It was the absence of this love, Rousseau believed, that produced the "wicked slaves" willing to exploit the laws for their selfish advantage he saw everywhere in the contemporary society. (1755b:1987, p. 124)

The state education must start at the earliest possible age:

> "(…) early enough never to consider their own persons except in terms of being related to the body of the state, and not to perceive their own existence except as part of the state's existence ... It is too late to alter our natural inclinations when they have taken their course and habit has been joined with self-love ... It is from the first moment of life that one must learn to deserve to live." (p. 125)

The principle is to 'catch them young'. The statement, however, is startling for the reader who has read Rousseau's pronouncements about freedom in the earlier *Discourses*. The principle about the lasting influence of our early upbringing restates that already expressed as early as in the *Project*, will be echoed in *Emile*, and corresponds with today's wisdom. But the first part of the statement unambiguously directs schools to indoctrinate children from their earliest years to identify themselves totally with the state, and this is troubling to the modern democratic mind, no matter his declared commitment to freedom, because it sounds, and is, totalitarian. The second part, which ends with the statement that "one must learn to deserve to live," is also troubling to today's mentality attuned rather to the language of the *right* to live, and to the politics of state welfare.

One wonders where the family, so much celebrated in the *Second Discourse* for its crucial educational role – "morality and marital fidelity," he says in the *Confessions*, "are at the root of all social order" – features in this account of things? (1770:1953, p. 405) The indications are that in an ideal world, where families perform their proper social and political function, Rousseau would have had *them* performing the task of educating their children rather than public schools. But his was not an ideal world; he had no confidence in the ability of the present families to educate their children responsibly. "Children cannot be abandoned to the lights and prejudices of their fathers," he says, the same argument he made to justify foregoing the upbringing of his own children. (p. 125) The Romans were the only people who could dispense with public schooling because "they made all their homes so many schools for children." (p. 126) The success of Roman home education, however, depended on severe paternal authority, and he disapproved of severe government, of individual or society, personally, pleading for wisdom instead. In *Emile*, as we shall see, the Tutor is not the boy's father, and the boy is raised outside any family ambit.

The principles of public instruction in the Third Discourse are confirmed in *Poland* written sixteen years later in 1771. At the start of this, the bleakest time in his life, he could still be optimistic that the virtues of citizenship, of spiritual vigour, patriotic zeal, and high public esteem he so admired in the ancients (as he enumerated them himself) were not completely lost to European society. Indeed, he was still confident that "the leaven they used is present in the hearts of all men," and only awaits the political institutions that would revive them. (1771:1985, p. 23) These institutions were what he sought to give the Poles, who were promising subjects because they were reasonably sheltered from the "exposure to corrupt teachings, outmoded institutions, and a philosophy of egoism that preaches and kills," that infected their European neighbours. (p. 23) True they had never yet "felt the true yoke of laws" and the country's size, difficult geography and complicated political history added to their political problems. On the other hand, their conservative, idiosyncratic, traditions and customs were "too deeply rooted to be stifled by new plantings," (1771:1985, p. 1) and a strong nationalistic and near-anarchic sense of independence guarded them from the modernizers among them who would have them re-model their constitution on the lines of the leading countries in Europe, all of which were, in Rousseau's belief, "hastening to their doom." (p. 2) But, for these very reasons, they combined the "stability of an ancient people and the docility of a new people," required by the *Social Contract* and were therefore ideal to receive a constitution *de novo*. (1762a:1987, p. 168) All the Polish institutions needed, in his view, was an overhaul that would make them workable and just.

In *Poland*, unlike in the *Third Discourse*, he devotes a whole section to education. He begins by reaffirming his belief that nothing but the law should hold "sway over the hearts of the citizens," and that they must internalize its authority as theirs. (1771:1985, p. 4) As in the *Third Discourse*, he describes the political object of public schooling as "to shape the souls of the citizens in a national pattern," and so to direct the opinions of the students "that they shall be patriotic by inclination, passionately, of necessity." (p. 19) Again, he advocates catching the children very young: "The newly-born infant, upon first opening his eyes, must gaze upon the fatherland, and until his dying day should behold nothing else." (p. 19) The souls of the citizens are 'shaped' with the games they play in infancy at home and the instruction they receive at school in their childhood. The 'shaping' will continue when they are adults, with their participation in public rituals and festivities, games, festivals, competitions, and so on; activities where the spirit of friendship and solidarity comes to the fore through the experience of conviviality, and the sense of community is reaffirmed and strengthened. Rousseau recognises the educational value of such participation not just in *Poland*; he encourages it elsewhere in his writing, in the *Second Discourse* and *Heloise*, for instance. The consolidation of the patriotic bond that ties the citizens together also requires an institutionalised religion, also with its own public rituals and activities.

A "truly national education," he insists in *Poland*, must be patriotic in this way. It must make the growing child "a Pole, not some other kind of man." Already, at the age of ten he:

"should be familiar with everything Poland has produced; at twelve to know all its provinces, all its roads, all its towns; at fifteen, to have mastered his country's entire history, and at sixteen, all its laws; let his mind and heart be

15

full of every noble deed, every illustrious man, that ever was in Poland so that he can tell you about them at a moment's notice." (p. 20)

How he understands freedom is evident in his claim that this sort of education "belongs only to men who are free." One is free, by implication, when one does one's patriotic duty, and doing one's patriotic duty is how one is free. (p. 20) The system of public instruction, he continues, again along the lines of the *Third Discourse*, must be administered with supreme authority by a board of top-grade officials, and "the content, the sequence, even the method of their studies," will "be specified by Polish law." In short, no significant control or pedagogical initiative is allowed the teachers or the schools, everything is determined for them by the state – as with any totalitarian system. In order to tighten the patriotic agenda further, only Polish nationals would be allowed to teach in the schools and these would be married men of distinction publicly recognised for "their conduct, their probity, their good sense, and their lights." After years of creditable service in teaching they would be retired and promoted to more prestigious and less-exacting posts in the state. "Above all else," he advises the Poles, not to "make the mistake of turning teaching into a career," because careers are tied with ambition, prestige, and reward, in short, they encourage *amour-propre* – teaching should be regarded as a service given by friends. Indeed, the state should recognise no other career than citizen. All should be citizens without distinction operating within a fluid meritocratic system which encourages them to seek their own advancement to the more important positions in their society out of a spirit of service. This is how the state "can unlock a great storehouse of energy," that is the human resources of its citizens while recognising their equality as citizens. (p. 20)

Though he follows on Plato's view that public schools must be supervised closely by the state, Rousseau does not follow Plato's system of universal compulsory education for males and females in co-educational settings. His public schools would be affordable for "the poor nobles," and there would be "scholarships" for children of "poor gentlemen" deserving reward for their service to the fatherland. They would be regarded as "'wards of the fatherland'." Rousseau repeats the emphasis on the value of physical education in *Poland* he had made already in *Emile*; the same emphasis made before him by Plato and Locke. Moreover his key pedagogical principle remains the same: "I cannot repeat too often," he says in *Poland*, "that good education must always be negative education," an education aimed to "choke off the vices before they are born." (p. 21) Children must be encouraged to be constantly active and to play together in a healthy spirit of competition and emulation. Parents must be made to participate in their activities and to continue with them at home. Besides its physical benefits, playing games contributes positively to the moral and political formation of children, introducing them "to rules, to equality, to fraternity, to competition, to living with the eyes of their fellow-citizens upon them and to seek public approbation," which will be their reward for their deeds and qualities. (p. 22)

With this last statement one wonders what has happened to his frequent warning against *amour-propre* which is exactly what tends to be fuelled by the desire for acclamation and the emulation of others. The answer is that Rousseau did not regard *amour-propre* (vying for the approval of others) as such, as bad *in itself* or intrinsically disordered, to the contrary he saw it as a necessary social sentiment required by any human relationship, and therefore as natural to social beings as their distress with the suffering of their fellows. Not only did he not consider the two sentiments of *amour de soi* and *amour-propre* as "exclusive and opposed," to the contrary he considered a healthy form of the latter, properly tempered with virtue, to be complementary with the former. (1755b:1987, p. 106) What he criticised as unhealthy was the kind of narcissistic and self-centred *amour-propre* he saw everywhere around him, which he identified with vanity, dishonesty, and superficiality, and which was not to be confused with *amour de soi*. For Rousseau the sentiment of *amour de soi*, or self-love, articulates itself as 'care for oneself' which was the exclusive care for pre-social man, but in a social setting care for oneself must take into account one's care for others and the way it needs to be re-defined is as self-mastery.

THE STATE AS EDUCATOR

Given this importance he attributes to it in the *Third Discourse* and later in *Poland*, the question must arise: why is there no discussion, or even mention, of institutionalized public instruction or schools (this "most important business" of the state as he calls it) in the *Social Contract*? One could speculate that he assumed that the citizens in the state of the *Social Contract* would be educated on the lines of the *Third Discourse*. (Wiborg 2000, pp. 236–237) But why is this intention not explicitly stated in the text of the *Social Contract*, or indeed in any foot-note? A credible alternative reason, it seems to me, is that he thought schooling unnecessary for the ideally governed state of the *Social Contract*. Emile also, as we shall see, is not sent to school, but in *Emile*, as in the *First Discourse*, Rousseau tells us why; the current educational institutions, he says, cannot be trusted to educate the patriotic sentiments of the young, because the very idea of a fatherland had been expunged from the contemporary mind. They are "laughable establishments," he says, capable only of creating selfish men in conflict with themselves and with their fellows, who end their days "without having been good either for ourselves or for others." (1762b:1991, p. 41)

His writing on public schooling in the *Third Discourse* could be taken to constitute his views on the kind of reform they would require to become serious institutions capable of educating their students effectively as patriotic citizens. But education through institutionalized public schooling seems always to have been a second option for Rousseau necessary where political entities that are so large and complex as to be intrinsically ungovernable in any other politically legitimate way, nation states like France and England (and Poland) for instance, are concerned. Things are different with small city-states like Geneva, then with a total population of a mere 20,000 persons, of whom only 1,500 were actually citizens and burgesses. (Cranston 1983, p. 15) These, as we saw in the letter preceding the *Second Discourse*, he regarded as the ideal political setting for a well-governed state, the state of the *Social Contract*. As we saw, what he visualised there was a community of healthy patriarchal families intimate to the point of being incestuous, bound together by a patriotism of *fraternal friendship* where one's love of country translates into love for one's fellow citizens. Such a society has no need for institutionalised state instruction; the education of the citizens takes care of itself. It comes first from the family then from living in the community and in the state. The opposite is true of societies incapable of this close community, large and complex societies where patriotism can be experienced only at the relatively abstract level of love for country, and specialised institutions are required to educate children into it. As Reisert points out, Rousseau regarded the uniting sentiment of friendship as beyond bourgeois society where no "'sincere friendships; no … real esteem; no … well-founded trust' (D1 8)," was possible because a narcissistic culture of *amour-propre* dominated people's lives. (2003, p. 78) Friendship is an emotional attachment which proceeds from our natural inclination to empathise with others and which, Rousseau believed, requires the availability of convivial events and occasions, the festivals, games, ceremonies, and so on, mentioned earlier, where people mix and enjoy themselves together, which is only possible for small intimate communities.

A society of well-ordered families held together by patriotic ties expressed in the sentiments of brotherly friendship shared between its citizens and a love of virtue, and a state ordered politically by the politics of the general will overseen by a wise Legislator or educator, has no need for independent institutions of instruction, it educates itself. But where did such a society exist? Where did such families exist? Rousseau had lost faith in Geneva and in contemporary families that were built on "ill-formed relationships that are the result of our civil order." (1755a:1987, p. 92) A new start was needed; the education of a new man and woman, the education prescribed in *Emile* which, it will be remembered, was written concurrently with the *Social Contract*. These would educate a new ideal household, the household of *Heloise*, which would be the building block for the new society which existed only in theory so far, the society of the *Social Contract*.

SUMMARY AND COMMENT

Rousseau's political works from the critique of the *First Discourse* to the *Social Contract*, describing a transition from men-as-they-are in the contemporary society to men-as-they-could-be if they lived with the appropriate laws and institutions, forms a coherent project which is continuous with *Emile* and *Heloise* the subjects of the next chapter. *Heloise*, as we shall see, is about the politics of domestic education, *Emile* about the politics of the one-to-one relationship between boy and Tutor. Since he equates education with government, his political project is concurrently educational, hence there is no distinction between the two processes in his thought. In this chapter we saw him identifying patriotism as the political aim of the education of the citizen and advocating a tight, state-controlled, institutionalised system of public instruction for the purpose of achieving it; in the *Third Discourse* first then in *Poland*. I suggested that these political/educational works reveal what could be described as a pragmatic Rousseau responding to the challenge of re-animating the sentiment of patriotism among his fellow citizens lost in the contemporary European reality of large complex nation-states like France, England, and Poland and bourgeois societies. The idealistic Rousseau, on the other hand, dispenses with such institutions. He reveals himself first in his outline description of an ideal political unit, a state of families he would choose to live in, in the *Second Discourse*, then provides its full political description in the *Social Contract* where education proceeds directly from the state and the family without intermediary institutions.

It is not difficult, given the contrary tendencies in his political thought that have emerged in our account, to understand why some "regard him as champion of both educational and political freedom," while others sense "an authoritarian strain in his thought," and suggest "that the seeds of modern totalitarianism are found in his writing." (Carbone 1985, p. 399) The conflicting views, as we shall see, will extend to *Emile* which Compayre, for instance, claimed "inspired the democratic idea of making instruction general," (1908:2002, p. 74) William Boyd that it "gives modern education a fresh orientation in the direction of democracy," (1968, p. 178) Reisert that it constitutes "the democratic reply to *The Republic*," (2003, p. 25) and Tal Gilead that it promotes "the happiness and welfare of the individual as an educational goal," and inspires the development of individualistic trends in modern education. (2005:427) But these judgments do not square with what we have seen him say about the aims of public schooling in the *Third Discourse* and *Poland*. Oksenberg Rorty has described the *Social Contract* accurately as "an egalitarian transformation of Plato's *Republic*" where Plato's ideal of "a philosophically determined rational order" ruled by philosopher experts is replaced with an ideal of a "rational individual autonomy" which must, however, coincide perfectly with the collective conscience. (1998, p. 247)

In this way, as Peter Gay has put it, Rousseau wanted "to reconcile the irreconcilable, the design of totalitarian democracy." (1987, p. vii) Indeed, the fact is that, like his mentor Plato, Rousseau revered order and regarded it as valuable above all else; "man cannot find happiness in disorder," he claimed, "rather it is when there is order that he is able to enjoy true happiness. To live in a state of disorder is to lead a life of misery." (Viroli 2002, p. 29) As Gay says, reconciling his instinct for freedom with this obsession with order within a single political theory that accommodates both doesn't work, in modern eyes at least. It is easy to see why. "The good man," Rousseau says elsewhere, "orders himself in relation to the whole, and the wicked orders the whole in relation to himself," and one is not free to be wicked; if necessary the collective must *force* its freedom on the individual. (Dent 2005, p. 111) This is a paradox the modern liberal democrat cannot live with. This "ordering" of the individual "in relation to the whole" is, as we have seen, what he wants the institutions of instruction, or schools, set up by the state, to do in the name of education, from the earliest years of childhood, so that as citizens they will "never to consider their own persons except in terms of being related to the body of the state," and they will not "perceive their own existence except as part of the state's existence," and to "shape(s) the soul of citizens in a national pattern." And these, undoubtedly, describe the political agenda not of a democratic but of a totalitarian state.

His distinction of 'the man' from the citizen creating a private sphere where individual freedom is beyond state or collective interference sounds, and indeed is, distinctly liberal. On the other hand he continues to define the private sphere negatively as what remains after the common good, or good of the community, has been defined with laws. It is always clear in his writing that consideration of the common good takes precedence over those of freedom, which is residual to how comprehensively that good is defined, a matter for the collective to decide, and this is consistent with his communitarian outlook. "Were there a people of gods," he says in the *Social Contract*, "it would govern itself democratically," which is to say that "so perfect a government is not suited to men." (1762a:1987, p. 180) It is more possible to find divine qualities in a single man, a Legislator, than it is to find in a whole people – but then Rousseau insists that the Legislator, who does possess divine qualities, must not be confused with a benevolent dictator on the Platonic model. As Maurizio Viroli says, "It is not possible to analyse the theory of political order in Rousseau's work independently of his conception of natural order and his doctrine of moral order." (2002, p. 17) This conception, and the totalitarian strains in Rousseau's writing, were very much the result of his theology described in his *Confessions* and, by proxy (as we shall see in the next chapter), by the Savoyard Vicar, premised on his view of the natural world as perfectly ordered to a divine plan conceived by the inscrutable mind of an infinitely wise and benevolent Creator/ architect, and his conviction that the model of the natural order must be imitated by the political/educational order as the framework for civil and political society. The edifice of his politics relies on the credibility of this thinking which has little purchase in today's secular modern/postmodern world.

CHAPTER ONE QUESTIONS

1. In the *First Discourse* Rousseau attacks the contribution of the sciences and the arts to the European Enlightenment civilization of his time, implying that their inclusion in the school curriculum contributed to the general state of degeneration of the society. How would you have defended yourself against these charges were you one of the *philosophes* of the time? How would you evaluate the importance of the sciences and the arts for today world?
2. Discuss (a) the importance Rousseau gives to patriotism as an educational aim and (b) his curriculum to achieve it in public schools. How relevant should patriotism be as an aim in today's curriculum?
3. Rousseau is generally taken to have followed Plato in recommending the establish-ment of state educational systems in the *Third Discourse*. Critically compare his system there and in *Poland* with Plato's in *The Republic*.

EDUCATION DOMESTIC AND SOLITARY

Emile and Heloise

"Whoever suffices to himself does not want to harm anyone at all." (*Rousseau, Judge of Jean-Jacques: Dialogues*, finished 1776 published posthumously, italics in original, Masters & Kelly 1990, p. 100).

THE PUBLICATION OF *EMILE*

Rousseau began to write *Emile* in 1758 when he was already working steadily on *Heloise*. Having severed his connections with Paris, his newly-found "leisure and independence" enabled him to write regularly and undisturbed and to produce his best and most lasting works. (1770:1953, p. 466) The year following, he conceived of and began compiling material for the *Confessions*; a work, he promised, that would be "unique and unparalleled in its truthfulness." (p. 478) In the winter of 1760 *Heloise* was finally finished and dispatched to his publisher Rey in Amsterdam. The book caused a stir in the Paris salons even before its publication in January 1761 when it immediately became a success and made him a lot of money. "Opinions differed among men of letters," he writes, but "in the world the verdict was unanimous, and the women especially were wild about the book and its author." (p. 504)

Now, while the writing of *Emile* was proceeding well, he was extracting "whatever could be extracted" from his abandoned work on *Political Institutions* to write the *Social Contract*, and working occasionally on a *Dictionary of Music*. (p. 478) However, his condition growing increasingly closer to paranoia with time, he became convinced that his enemies were circulating bogus works in his name to blacken and discredit him. Rey had the *Social Contract* out quickly in April 1762. *Emile*, however, which was to be his "last and best work," was a different story. Its publisher, Duchesne, dragged his feet mysteriously. (p. 523) Unauthorised selections from it began to appear abroad, and he offered the author no explanation for the delay. Rousseau suspected plots on all sides and the hand of the Jesuits. He became "disturbed by vague and melancholy presentiments," when he began receiving "rather strange" reports and letters, some signed and others anonymous. (p. 521) The book finally appeared in print in May of 1762, a month or so after the *Social Contract*. Meanwhile, earlier that year, he had written the *Letters to Malesherbes* (his first published autobiographical material) straight off without revision, "containing the true picture of my character and the true motives for all my behaviour," and anticipating the *Confessions*. (Kelly et al. 1995, p. 572)

The guarded comments of his friends and the unsigned letters of congratulation from literati that followed *Emile*'s publication were "the dull murmurings that precede the storm" – that soon broke. (1770:1953, p. 531) In July of that same year the book was condemned publicly in an edict by the Archbishop of Paris Christophe de Beaumont. That same month he received the devastating news of *Maman*'s death. A "darkness in which I have been entombed for eight years past, without ever having been able, try as I might, to pierce its hideous obscurity," he wrote later, engulfed him. (p. 543) The real persecution he was to suffer for the rest of his life began at this time as he found himself being relentlessly driven from town to town, city to city, country to country, frequently in disguise, by his enemies. With it grew the tone of bitterness in his writing which begins with his *Letter to Christophe Beaumont*, published in May 1763, in which he replied to the archbishop's edict.

HELOISE: ON DOMESTIC EDUCATION

Rousseau represented both *Heloise* and *Emile* as 'novels', the first an epistolary one; i.e. one written in the form of an exchange of letters. Julie l'Etange is its hero, St Preux is her tutor who becomes her lover. Their passionate but ill-starred affair ends when it is discovered and Julie's father orders her to break it off because St Preux is of inferior social rank and she is promised to his friend an M. de Wolmar. When Julie ends their liaison St Preux contemplates suicide but is persuaded by Lord Edward Bomston, his friend and protector, to travel the world instead. Returning from his travels years after he contacts Claire, Julie's close cousin and confidante, to discover that Julie has married Wolmar and they have a young family. He is astonished soon after to receive a courteous letter from Wolmar himself informing him that he knew of his affair with Julie and inviting him to stay at their house, Clarens. St. Preux accepts the invitation with several, not unjustified, misgivings, because his passion for Julie is quickly re-kindled when they meet. But Julie overcomes a moment of strong crisis, a severe test to her marital fidelity set up by Wolmar, and stands firm. Her relationship with St. Preux now changes and is transformed into one of friendship as he comes to admire her qualities as a wife, mother, and mistress of the household. His respect for Wolmar deepens also, and the *menage a trois* echoes the friendship of twenty years earlier with Anet and *Maman* with the difference that Julie remains faithful to Wolmar, an "enlightened observer, who combined a father's interest with a philosopher's detachment." (1761:1997, p. 460) St. Preux is allowed into the intimate family circle and estate at Clarens, which is a self-contained domestic unit of which Wolmar is the architect and which Julie manages – a clear replica of the Legislator/Prince political model of the *Social Contract*. St. Preux's observations and reflections on the politics of the household, the children's education, and a host of other matters, are relayed to Lord Bomston in a series of long lively commentaries.

The Wolmars have two young sons, and Henriette, Claire's slightly older daughter, lives with them. The children's active upbringing is Julie's responsibility. On one occasion St. Preux sits with her and Wolmar after breakfast in Julie's room oberving the boys, lively, noisy, and thoughtless at play, "as befits their age." They grow increasingly boisterous and rowdy by the minute and St. Preux is disappointed that she does not intervene. He raises the subject with her when they are taken away by their nanny, upbraiding her gently for her inaction and making the point that discipline must not wait until their later years if she wants them to grow docile and obedient. Julie responds with the educational principles that will be familiar to the reader of *Emile*. The boys, she says, must be treated as children and allowed their natural freedom; being boisterous and uninhibited is how they express and enjoy it. Instruction will follow later when they are ready for it. Were they argumentative and defiant it would be another matter, but such attitudes come not with freedom but with boredom. Their readiness to learn must be respected always and, at this age, their physical development must be a priority. They must not be subjected to any regime of books or study that makes for a sedentary life. The uniqueness of their temperament and natural genius must be respected, not "changed nor constrained, but formed and perfected." Nature makes us all "good and sound," a bad education is what turns us vicious, she concludes her little lecture, anticipating the opening lines of *Emile*. (p. 461)

Later, on the same lines, Wolmar rejects St. Preux's suggestion that children should be educated on the model of a properly educated man on the grounds that it means trying to "correct nature." (p. 462) St. Preux replies that maybe we are not so much the work of nature as of our upbringing and that, this being the case, our education should be about *forming* our minds on a desirable model not about non-interference with our natural growth. Rousseau thus anticipates a powerful argument against his fundamental assumption that we are made good by nature, i.e. that we are not what nature but what society makes us. Wolmar, speaking with Rousseau's voice, draws St. Preux's attention to two puppies from the same litter and never separated since birth, playing in the courtyard, in reply; one is smart and lively the other sluggish and dull. Again St. Preux's rejoinder is pertinent: one cannot conclude from the fact that they were raised together that their upbringing was identical, he points out, for no two experiences ever are, even if they appear to be. Wolmar's reply is lame and somewhat disappointing. Given that we have no accurate knowledge of the working of a child's mind, he says, he would rather not play the "astrologer." He would rather stick to his observation and "leave aside all these subtleties." (p. 463) "To change a mind," he maintains, is "to change its inner organisation; to change a character you would have to change the temperament it depends on. So it would be vain to pretend to remodel a variety of minds on a common model." (pp. 463–464)

The discussion stops there, St. Preux appears to concede. But the conclusion is reasonable only if one accepts the questionable premises it follows from; i.e. that the mind has an 'inner organisation' and that one's temperament is natural not learnt (both of which were denied by the empiricists, for instance). On the other hand the claim that one cannot "remodel a variety of minds on a common model" seems to conflict with his view on education, just discussed, that the individual minds of citizens can be taught to conform without violence with a model of patriotic citizenship, but that, as we have seen, is another story driven by a different political plot. It also seems to conflict with *Emile* where the tutor is an obvious model for the growing boy. Interestingly, Julie herself seems to disagree with her husband on this matter since she declares that she is raising her boys to be like their father. Wolmar goes on to pronounce the principle that grounds the pedagogical philosophy of *Emile*, that to educate is not to "change the character and bend the natural disposition, but on the contrary to push it as far as it can go, to cultivate it and prevent it from degenerating." This is the principle of *negative education*, which, as I remarked earlier, Rousseau re-defines in different contexts and which is key to *Emile*. It is thus that "man becomes all he can be, and [that] nature's work is culminated in him by education," Wolmar concludes. (p. 464)

St. Preux's reply echoes Rousseau's claim in the *Third Discourse* that the civil state cannot afford this understanding of education because it must harness the talents of its citizens for its prosperity as it does its material resources. And this requires training regimes that bend their "natural disposition" into loyalty towards the state and their fellow citizens and to the purposes of economic productiveness. The discussion has grown intriguing at this point, but Rousseau stops it there. He has, however, raised the question that lies at the heart of *Emile* and the *Social Contract*, and of modern education in general; how do you educate in a manner that allows unrestricted individual growth *and* satisfies the demands of governance and the interests of society? How do you reconcile individual freedom with the common good? Wolmar announces another thesis in *Emile* that the mind's cultivation should be postponed until such time when the body and the senses have matured already and the child is ready for it. But St. Preux puts this thesis to interrogation too. And again Wolmar replies by practical example; he points this time to his own children happily at play and untroubled by any kind of intellectual exertion. The answer appears to satisfy St. Preux but, given the boys' very tender ages how can one be confident that the price they would pay for their present happiness is not any long term harm? Today's wisdom holds that the child's physical, emotional, and cognitive growth is concurrent not sequential. As Compayre puts it: "If Emile's intellect lies fallow for twelve years, it will be like those fields which the husbandman does not sow: weeds will spring up in alarming abundance; and when their destruction is desired, it will be too late." (1908:2002, p. 27) The secret of the child's upbringing as a free man Rousseau says in *Heloise*, again anticipating *Emile*, is to replace "the yoke of discipline," which is external, with "the yoke of necessity," which is internal. (1761:1997, p. 465) The Wolmars let their boys run freely with the peasants, building their bodily strength and endurance in the process, and learning to be fearless and independent without, however, being self-indulgent or domineering over their social inferiors. Achieving this is "effortless" for them in a house where "the relationship between servants and masters is but an exchange of services and attentions," and where the politics of the household (as they are intended in the wider society of the *Social Contract*) are based on "reciprocal affection, born of equality." (p. 468)

EMILE: THE EDUCATION OF THE MAN

In the Preface to the first edition of *Emile* Rousseau refers to the book modestly as a "collection of reflections and observations, disordered and almost incoherent," first intended as a monograph of a few pages that grew uncontrollably into "a sort of opus. Too big doubtless, for what it contains, but too small for the matter that it treats." (1762b:1991, p. 33) Later, as we saw, he was to describe it as the culmination of his work, continuous with the *Discourses* and with the *Social Contract*, intended for educated reading, but written by "a simple man, a friend of the truth." A book "founded less on principles than on facts," (p. 110) but, at the same time, "a visionary's dreams about education," describing "the goal that must be set," but not claiming that it can be reached, only that "he who comes nearest to it will have succeeded best." (p. 95) By practical he means possible to accomplish "wherever men are." (p. 35) He dismisses any suggestion that he would have been better occupied describing possible reforms to current educational practices because these practices, he says, were fundamentally flawed and beyond any reform or redemption. (p. 34) The only way forward is to re-define education *de novo*, for a new kind of man for a new kind of society. In short, he promises his reader nothing less than a work which is revolutionary.

However, as I remarked earlier, he continues to define education consistently with the *Third Discourse* as "the art of forming men," i.e. of governance, and the "first of all useful things," but still largely neglected excluding Locke's work. (p. 33) *Emile* opens with Rousseau's article of faith and substantially the same premise as the *Social Contract*. "Everything is good as it leaves the hands of the Author of things. Everything degenerates in the hands of man," *but* (and this is an important 'but' which answers to the mistaken interpretations of Rousseau as radically anti-social) without civil society things would be "even worse." (p. 37) It consists of five 'Books' distinguishing three phases of Emile's education: first into a natural and self-sufficient; then into a social and moral; and finally into a civic and political, being. The Fourth Book, as indicated earlier, includes the 'Profession of Faith of the Savoyard Vicar' and the Fifth, the last, addresses the education of Sophie, 'the woman'.

We get our education Rousseau says, signifying his broad use of the word, "from nature or from men or from things." (p. 38) The infant child must be treated as a "nascent shrub" and nurtured in accordance with its intrinsic nature, not formed or forced into a shape by the direct intervention of an adult. The first injunction for the Tutor (as for the Legislator for a society before giving it its constitution), is to study one's pupil. These ideas anticipated, as we saw, in *Heloise* were already radical for his time. More radical for us today is his view that a boy must be educated as a self-sufficient solitary first before he can be made a moral and social being and a citizen. (p. 39) Our view today, in our age of mass schooling, is the contrary; we assume that we need to socialise children first, in a family then at school, before we encourage them to have minds of their own, and that their moral development is an intrinsic part of this upbringing. We are, therefore, even more intrigued to discover that Emile's education is not, like the Wolmar children, to be in a domestic setting because, as was observed earlier, although Rousseau theorised an ideal domestic education in *Heloise* he believed that parents in his society had lost the ability to raise their children since they were at odds "both about the order of their functions and about their system." (p. 48) The women were especially to blame for this; were they to be true mothers "men will soon become fathers and husbands again." (p. 46) But they were more interested in "the entertainments of the city" than in raising their families, or indeed in having families.

(p. 44) The occasional brave soul who revolted against this regime was quickly put down by her own sex.

When the father took over his six or seven year old son's upbringing he found an "artificial seed" already formed. Then he compounded the matter by teaching him everything except to know himself and to live and be happy. Finally, the young man was cast into the world "frail in body and soul alike." (p. 48) Hence, while mothers fail in their duty to provide society with moral and virtuous men, fathers fail to provide it with "sociable men." (p. 49) It was in reaction against this situation that the pedagogy of *Emile* evolved, both with regards the education of the boy and, more indirectly, of the girl Sophie – the book is really, as I remarked earlier, about the education of a new family to start a new society. "To make a man," Rousseau declares, a Tutor must be "more than a man himself," he must be a "rare mortal," like the Legislator, or Wolmar, or indeed Anet. (pp. 49–50) So Emile's tutor is not his father but a "friend" of this kind. Rousseau, probably recalling his unhappy experience with the Mably children and his own failure as a father, acknowledges that he is not such a man himself – but this does not mean that he is unqualified to describe the pedagogy such a man should pursue.

Emile is an imaginary child of average intelligence, physically robust and healthy, not of noble rank but not poor either since "a poor man does not need to be educated. His station gives him a compulsory education," always understanding 'governance' by the term. (p. 52) He is raised without family or friends even, in a temperate climate and in the quiet of a rustic environment, since "cities 'are the abyss of the human species'," dens that breed vice, and the success of the first part of his education depends on his avoiding any contact with vice. (p. 59) His tutor is his guardian and constant companion. He begins to learn with the first days of life; "before speaking, before understanding," he is "already learning." (p. 62) His early education will teach him "always to be master of himself and in all things to do his will, as soon as he has one." (p. 63) This could appear a recipe for rebelliousness, self-centredness and a dominating personality but, as we shall see, this is very far from Rousseau's intention. Affirming Locke's empiricist belief that the child's "sensations are the first materials of his knowledge," he deduces that an education that follows nature must begin with the cultivation of the senses. (p. 64) So Emile is encouraged to explore his environment freely exercising all his senses in the process. His tutor intervenes only when he is threatened with serious harm or self-injury. His early infantile cries of distress, expressions of "want and weakness," create the social bond with his tutor, who will ignore them except when the boy is sick or needlessly frustrated. (p. 65) They also activate his sentiment of *amour-propre* through his wish to please his tutor. He receives nothing directly from his tutor nor is his will frustrated when he wants something. Thus, he is disposed neither to dominion nor to rebellion. Rousseau attributes the wantonness and destructiveness of early childhood to his weakness, and confidently predicts that they will disappear as his self-confidence grows with time and as he grows older. The maxim for his tutor at this age is to allow Emile "more true freedom and less domination." (p. 68)

Another is to give him time to mature, not to be too impatient or demanding with him, nor allow him to get ahead of himself, otherwise "a vice is planted in the depth" of his heart which it will be difficult to eradicate later. (p. 92) The form this strategy takes includes a measure we now know to be disastrous, (but then Rousseau was not cognisant of our theories of language acquisition and development), to restrict Emile's vocabulary as much as possible. He must not "have more words than ideas," nor will he "know how to say more things than he can think." (p. 74) As in *Heloise* the tutor is urged to respect Emile's childhood, to recognise its role "in the order of human life," (p. 80) not to "hurry to judge it, either for good or for ill," nor to frustrate its tendencies when they appear. (p. 107) The wise Tutor knows, like Wolmar, that "each mind has its own form," and will "let childhood ripen in children," rather than seek to short-circuit it with precocious knowledge, (p. 94) which (and Rousseau was evidently thinking of his own childhood) "is the cause of children's ruin." (p. 107) Emile's happiness at this stage comes, like that of the solitary pre-social savage, from that his "power and will [are] in perfect equality". (p. 80) This is what makes him 'well ordered', the scope of government/education. "The truly free man wants only what he can do and does what he pleases." This "fundamental maxim," Rousseau remarks, is the root of all the rules of education. (p. 84) Emile is discouraged by his experience from thinking himself capable of more than he can achieve, which is "the true source of all our miseries," and learns that to be truly free and happy is to live as fully as one can but within one's possibilities; to "remain in the place which nature assigns to you in the chain of being," and to accept suffering and death as one's human condition. (p. 83)

NEGATIVE EDUCATION: AFFIRMING *AMOUR DE SOI*

This principle of knowing one's place in the natural order is fundamental to Rousseau's politics of government/education; in a social context it translates into knowing one's place in the social/political order of the *Social Contract*. Meanwhile, mastery of speech brings Emile's infancy to a close. His experiences teach him the limitations of his powers and the consequences of his actions. His errors or misdemeanours are never punished. He breaks his window and the discomfort of living with it broken on cold nights tells him that it is a bad idea. He is not protected from pain and discomfort, but these are balanced by his tutor's "sweetness of commiseration," when he suffers. (p. 87) His moral education is negative. It consists not in "teaching virtue and truth but in securing the heart from vice and the mind from error." (p. 93) Rousseau describes negative education as the difficult art "of governing without precepts and doing everything by doing nothing." (p. 119) It is "difficult" because though it requires the Tutor not to intervene directly in the child's behaviour he must constantly "be the child's master," and never lose his control. (p. 95) The trick is to let his pupil "always believe he is the master, and let it always be you who are," to let him do what he wants but to make sure he wants to do only what you want. This is how the illusion of personal freedom coincides with the reality of governance in Rousseau's politics in general where the individual is required to internalize the will of his governor as the case may be. No subjection, he continues, ominously in virtue of what we said earlier about his disposition towards totalitarianism with the *Third Discourse*, is as perfect "as that which keeps the appearance of freedom," for "thus the will itself is made captive." (p. 120) Naked power, for Rousseau, is cruel and barbaric and, contrary to what Niccolo Machiavelli said, an inefficient way of rendering men docile because it leaves the will resentful and rebellious; for such efficiency the only tool is an education which makes the will captive.

Rousseau describes the age from birth to twelve as "the most dangerous period of human life" because errors made then and vices acquired are lasting. To be the child's master, according to the principle of negative education, means being "the master of all that surrounds him," natural and social. (p. 95) Emile's social environment must be controlled to limit human contact other than with his tutor in this pre-social stage despite "strong and solid", possibly "insurmountable," objections to this practice, and despite the acknowledged human failings of his tutor. (p. 94) The cultivation of his *amour de soi*, which is the basis of his education to this point, teaches Emile that his first duty is to himself, hence his sense of justice will be limited early to what is owed to him. Introduction to the socially important notion of property will teach him that there is also a justice owed to others. His tutor encourages him to cultivate a patch of beans in the garden. One morning he finds it uprooted. In distress he turns to his tutor for justice. The gardener is sent for. He admits to destroying the crop but complains that he had already planted the patch with melons himself, a more valuable product, and that *his* work was destroyed with the cultivation of the beans. Evidently, the whole business is a charade from beginning to end. Emile is set up by his tutor and there are other incidents in the book where he learns important lessons in a similar, stage managed, way.

The "only lesson of morality appropriate to childhood, and the most important for every age," more important than encouraging him to do good, which everyone to some degree does, is "never to harm anyone," oneself included. (p. 104) During this time he learns only his native language, but he speaks it well. He does not learn to study or memorize 'facts' since, Rousseau says, this exercise would be meaningless and boring for him. He learns only what he finds interesting; what he fails to show any interest in will not be forced on him. He is kept away from books, the instrument of children's "greatest misery," being valuable neither as objects of pleasure nor of instruction. They teach us "to use the reason of others … to believe much and never to know anything." (p. 125) Emile will only receive his first book to read when he is aged twelve, appropriately enough *Robinson Crusoe*. Learning to write, when he is ready for it, will follow. (p. 116) His physical education remains an integral part of his curriculum since the self-sufficient man needs an active mind and body, such as are harmonized in the agile and mentally nimble savage who Emile resembles at this time. At twelve he dresses comfortably but lightly, runs barefoot in all seasons to harden his skin and his resistance to the elements, sleeps long hours in order to fuel his energy, in a comfortable but not luxurious bed, swims as naturally and well as he walks and runs, and does nothing rashly. Sports and games hone his senses and skills. He can sing and play an instrument well, but does not yet read music. He prefers natural food and avoids meat, which "is not natural to man." (p. 153) Rousseau calls the "well-regulated" use of all his senses he has achieved at the time "common sense." It "resides only in the brain," in the form of "*perceptions* or *ideas*," and is still "*sensual* or *childish*;" the conjunction of several simple ideas. (p. 157)

His tutor, on his part, is "wholly involved with the child," watchfully anticipating the patterns of his growth, discouraging or encouraging them as the case may be. (p. 189) Emile is a "bubbling, lively, animated," child untroubled by any "gnawing cares, without long and painful foresight, whole in his present being, and enjoying a fullness of life which seems to want to extend itself beyond him." (p. 159) He has grown healthy, independent, alert, and fearless but not rash, and he seeks assistance only when he truly needs it. "Vulgar eyes see only a little rascal," in him, Rousseau remarks tellingly, clearly anticipating criticism, but "clear-sighted men" immediately recognise his true worth. (p. 162) The passions, a new danger, begin to make their appearance as he approaches early adolescence. The sexual are "the most terrible," of all. (p. 165) They cannot long be suppressed, but they must be kept at bay for as long as possible because their intrusion announces the end of this unique and precious time when his entire life was ruled by a self-indulgent *amour de soi*, and the intrusion of the sentiment of *amour-propre*. The guiding principle of his education must now change from self-indulgence to utility still measured, for the time being, in terms of his own "security, his preservation, and his well being," i.e. of his *amour de soi*. (p. 187) The tutor must match this change of focus with a changed relationship with his pupil; "the master's severity must succeed the comrade's compliance," as the need for external discipline begins to show itself. (p. 175) It is time for him to acknowledge his own fallibility and limitations honestly with his pupil – and this will be his first act of self-disclosure to him.

BECOMING SOCIAL: TAMING *AMOUR-PROPRE*

Emile now learns the basic notions of physics and chemistry as they become useful to him, again directly from nature not from books. (p. 177) He learns not to confuse the truth with the opinions of men or the evidence of his senses, and to seek his own answers to the questions that trouble or intrigue him, persisting with them, learning from his errors – his tutor intervenes only when he is totally frustrated. His understanding is thereby "far clearer and far surer" than it would be from reading or from the direct instruction of a teacher. (p. 176) He learns to use his hands, as the first of all useful things; "If, instead of gluing a child to books, I bury him in a workshop, his hands work for the profit of his mind; he becomes a philosopher and believes he is only a labourer." (p. 177) Natural, pre-social, man did not need to work, his idleness was productive, but with social man idleness brings nothing but vice and ruin, hence, work is "an indispensable duty for social man." (p. 195) Emile learns to distinguish it from play as a serious undertaking. He learns an artisan's trade which will free him from the ties of rank or land, or the need to conform to the views of others, by giving him financial security and independence. He can choose his trade himself, providing it is healthy, hard, and dangerous, not sedentary, repetitive, or soft. His tutor learns it with him, dirtying his hands also, in an artisan's workshop from a master-craftsman. Emile learns about the convention of money and is made conscious of the importance of social and economic transactions in a discussion with his tutor on what it takes to produce a meal. His first lessons in his material self-preservation and self-reliance, and this introduction into social and economic transactions, are a preparation for his transition into the social world.

Now in his mid-teens he is encouraged to continue to seek the truth for himself and to avoid rash judgments, even if what meets his eye seems certain and obvious to him – the stick half dipped in the pond appears broken to his eye but turns out to be straight. (p. 205) Aged fifteen with a mind of his own and mentally and physically strong, he knows nothing yet of history, morals or metaphysics, nor has he learnt to think in abstract terms. This is where his education goes next. Having learnt to relate to material things in terms of utility he now needs to learn to relate to other human beings, and how to "order(s) all the affections of the soul according to these relations." (p. 219) In short, his social and moral education now begins. The sentiment of *amour-propre*, "a useful but dangerous instrument," is still weak in him because, thus far, the wish to please the other has been excited only by his tutor. But the changes happening in his body, his growing passions, the attraction to the other sex in particular, will change all this and his perfect happiness as "a solitary being" entirely self-concerned will soon be lost. (p. 221) His *amour-propre* will grow stronger and the sentiments of love, friendship, and accord, will meet with "dissensions, enmity and hate." (p. 215) His sexual curiosity is discouraged by his tutor for as long as possible but his questions on the subject are answered seriously and frankly. (p. 216)

He now needs to be sensitised to the distress, suffering, and death of his fellows-humans, in accordance with the general principle by which he has been educated so far, by being taken to observe it and discover it for himself, in the hospitals, poor houses, asylums, morgues, etc. of the city. The experience arouses his natural pity, and he learns to judge his own happiness in relation to that of the unfortunates he sees; i.e. he learns the important quality of fraternity. Because suffering knows no social distinctions, he learns "to love all men" the same and to dishonour no one. (p. 226) But, Rousseau warns, it must not be overdone otherwise it achieves the opposite effect. He learns from the over-indulgence of others, particularly the sexual, that "the sweetest habit of the soul consists in a moderation of enjoyment which leaves little opening for desire and disgust." (p. 229) He also learns about his fellow humans by studying their passions in history; i.e. through the classics (as Rousseau had learnt them himself). He learns that they judge "things which are neutral or which are at most of interest as entertainment," with their taste, and that their "needs" stem from their appetites, (p. 340) that "all the true models of taste are in nature," and that good taste "depends on good morals" and is ruined by vanity and extravagance. (p. 343)

Rousseau believed that taste, like everything else, is gendered; that a woman's taste is more acute "in physical things connected with the judgment of the senses," and a man's "in moral things that depend more on the understanding." Emile is taken to Paris which is a laboratory of experiments in taste in all its forms. His literary taste has been cultivated with his reading of Latin and Classical literature, "for the sole reason that the ancients, since they came first, are closest to nature, and their genius is more their own" than that of contemporary writers. (p. 343) Rousseau calls it "pure literature," and Emile is taught to distinguish it from the "sewers in the reservoirs of modern compilers, newspapers, translations, and dictionaries." (p. 343–344) The theatre, however, followed by poetry, not literature, is where "one learns so well the art of pleasing men and of interesting the human heart;" i.e. of *amour-propre*. (p. 344) Emile learns that true good taste corresponds not with the show and cleverness of a warped *amour-propre* but with the virtues of simplicity and modesty, and that pleasures are best enjoyed not alone but with like-minded friends. Indeed, that "exclusive pleasures are the death of pleasure," and that "true entertainments" are those one shares with others not at the theatre but at festivals, games, fairs, etc., like the Wolmars. (p. 354)

These are telling remarks against those who, as we shall see later, sustain that Rousseau intended Emile to be educated for solitude. Emile's debut in society, when it comes, is "simple and without brilliance." (p. 233) His early errors as he finds his feet are corrected patiently by his tutor who increases his vigilance on him to the extent of sleeping in his room "at the very least." (p. 333) He learns to hate violence and injustice with all his heart, love all "the true models of the beautiful, all the moral relations of beings, all the ideas of order," and rejoice in the happiness of others. (p. 335) At the same time he learns that he must remain his own man, "to recognize the voice of friendship," when it is genuine, and to reciprocate it, but to hold to his views and principles always. (p. 332) His demeanour is honest and forthright. He is serene and self-possessed, and detached, like "a likable foreigner," while always showing concern, and being civil and respectful in his dealings with others, no matter who and what they are. (p. 339) He speaks sensibly, sparingly and unaffectedly, with due care for what he says, adopting the same honesty and forthrightness in his speech towards all alike whatever their age and rank and avoiding all ostentation and conceit. In short, he is the man Rousseau idealised for himself in those fateful days of self-reconstitution after he published the *First Discourse*.

THE VICAR'S PROFESSION OF FAITH

Why, given Rousseau's deep religiosity, has Emile, now aged eighteen and old enough to think about a suitable spouse, not yet heard of religion, or even of God? His reply is in Book Four, the book that mainly got him into trouble with the religious and political authorities of his day. Following the pedagogical reasoning of the book it is obvious: "the obligation to believe assumes the possibility of doing so," he says. (p. 257) Only now does Emile possess the intellectual maturity his religious education requires. Only now is he capable of the "gradual and slow climb," the understanding of "purely intellectual ideas," especially the idea of God, needed before he takes the final "leap" of faith, "a giant step upward of which childhood is not capable and for which even men need many rungs especially made for them." (p. 255) The Vicar will provide the 'young man' he professes to with these "rungs," the rungs for his self-education. Indeed, Emile will not be indoctrinated into any of the official religions nor will he be exposed to the "pedant teaching" of catechism. (p. 257) His tutor's ultimate aim is to put him "in a position to choose the one to which the best use of his reason ought to lead him." (p. 260)

The confused and unhappy young man who the semi-fictional figure of the Vicar professes himself to is roughly Emile's age (and Rousseau's in Turin in 1728, when he was 'rescued' from a life of depravity by the Abbe Gaime). "You shall see me, if not as I am," the Vicar tells him in words that echo Rousseau's own in his *Confessions*, "at least as I see myself"; i.e. he offers the young man not truth but honesty. (p. 266) The Vicar's method is to expound his way through his intuitions about the natural world behind which he detects the 'will' of a Creator, a supreme 'intelligence' inscrutable to the human mind, the appropriate attitude towards which is to "lift myself up," to "meditate on You ceaselessly. The worthiest use of my reason is for it to annihilate itself before You" – as, in a political setting, the individual annihilates his reason before that of the general will. (p. 286) Then he moves on to the intuitions he has gained about himself by his self-examination.

A self-confessed autodidact like Rousseau himself, he defends the validity of the human conscience as a moral tool against the widespread objection that it is nothing but the work of 'prejudice'. Using *Port Royale* terminology he describes it instead as an "inner light," an "innate principle of justice and virtue" which is universally inherent to human being, (p. 289) and which "persists in following the order of nature against all the laws of men," (p. 267) "the voice of the soul," in the same way as "the passions are the voice of the body," (p. 286) a "divine instinct" and "infallible guide to good and bad which makes man like unto God." Born "from this double relation to oneself and to one's fellows," it needs no "terrifying apparatus of philosophy," (p. 290) its acts "are not judgments but sentiments, suitable to our nature." (p. 289) It is God's voice speaking plainly and directly to the human heart, so that "he who follows his conscience obeys nature and does not fear being led astray." (p. 287) It tells us to pity others, and makes towards virtue, which lies "in the love for order," (p. 291) a love which, as I pointed out earlier, the Legislator/Tutor shares with the Creator.

But while this "love of order," this "concert reigns among the elements," while the natural world is ordered according to God's plan, the Vicar observes, there is nothing but "chaos," and "evil on earth." (p. 278) Men abuse the free will God gave them, which is not freedom "to want what is bad for me," but to seek my goodness in His will. (p. 280) Goodness is "the love of order which produces order," while justice is "the love of order which preserves order." (p. 282) Echoing the critique of the first two *Discourses*, the Vicar speaks of "our fatal progress" with "its errors and vices," without which, he says, "everything is good." (p. 282) The wicked man, Rousseau repeats, orders "the whole in relation to himself," makes himself "the centre of all things" in defiance of the natural order which emanates from "the common centre, which is God." Man is "but the work and the instrument of the great Being who wants what is good, who does it," like the Legislator in the political setting of the *Social Contract*. Man's happiness and well-being lie in collaborating with His will. As a citizen in a political context it lies in collaborating with the will of the Legislator. "For what felicity," the Vicar asks rhetorically, "is sweeter than sensing that one is ordered in a system in which everything is good?" and placing one's confidence in a Divine justice that will come at the end of one's life? (p. 292) Indeed, while "Man's justice is to give each what belongs to him ... God's justice is to ask from each for an accounting of what He gave him," when he leaves this life. (p. 285)

As I have been observing, this theology is interpreted politically in the *Social Contract*. The Legislator is the state's creator and conscience; the great Being whose invisible presence lies at the centre of the political order that emanates from him by way of its laws and institutions. The happiness of the citizen lies in "sensing that one is ordered in a system in which everything is good," because it is ordered wisely for the common good by the general will. The young man, is "not yet depraved enough by vice to be in danger of choosing badly." The Vicar invites him to "make your own those of my sentiments which have persuaded you." (p. 311) This invitation to a personal creed seems to conflict with his other advice to "go back to your own country, return to the religion of your forefathers," and to "follow it in the sincerity of your heart, and never leave it again." (p. 311) But the conflict is only apparent because for Rousseau both are needed; a private and a public religion, one serving the man's relation with his Creator through his conscience, the other serving the citizen in conformity with the public religion which "prescribe(s) in each country a uniform manner of honouring God by public worship," and which is supported by the state. (p. 308) The public conscience which is the general will requires this support. If the public religion conflicts with the directives of one's personal conscience one should seek another place to live where the two are at least compatible. This is how the conflict, in his own case, between his private beliefs and his dutiful public conformity with the Catholic religion is justified in the *Confessions*. (1770:1953, p. 365) The Vicar's own heart is tranquil in this respect because he serves humble parishioners in a small parish where personal example and works of charity count for more than the complexities of theology and dogma.

THE EDUCATION OF THE WOMAN

"Emile is not made to remain always solitary," Rousseau declares, the time has now come to find him a mate. (1772b:1991, p. 327) His tutor preconditions his search by feeding him with a picture of the ideal woman he should look for, even if the match is not perfect – controlling his choice! He even names her for him; Sophie "augurs well. If the girl whom you choose does not bear it she will at least be worthy of bearing it." (p. 329) The girl he will eventually find will be 'Sophie' no matter her real name. Rousseau begins Book Five with the argument, already made in the *Second Discourse*, that natural or biological differences between the sexes should be reflected in their social and political roles, and that an ordered relationship requires that their roles be complimentary, with the one, the male, being "active and strong, the other passive and weak," the one made to dominate, the other "to please and to be subjugated." (p. 358) It follows that Sophie "ought not to have the same education" as Emile. (p. 363) In sum:

> "(...) the whole education of women ought to relate to men. To please men,
> to be useful to them, to make herself loved and honoured by them, to raise
> them when young, to care for them when grown, to counsel them, to console

them, to make their lives agreeable and sweet – these are the duties of women at all times, and they ought to be taught from childhood." (p. 365)

The task of teaching them falls to their mothers.

Obviously these words, as I remarked earlier, jar on modern ears, liberal and feminist especially, and with good reason, but the condemnations that have followed have not always been fair with him. One common misconception is that he wanted women to be no more than powerless objects of male satisfactions. Against it one notes the important social and political role he ascribed to them in the *Second Discourse* as "chaste guardians of mores and the gentle bonds of peace;" no mean task given the social and political importance he gives to the family unit. Julie, the protagonist of *Heloise*, is hardly a powerless object. Women have their own peculiar power to seduce and repulse men's passions, and this gives them the real dominance in their relationship with men, which is just as "nature wants it." (p. 360) Using it wisely, he repeats from the *Second Discourse*, a woman can guide her man to find his strength, his self-esteem, and his natural virtue. (p. 358) Her nimble mindedness and looks are also a woman's "weapons," (p. 364) and her guile, a "peculiar cleverness given to the fair sex," keeps her "his equal." Indeed, in real terms, it is she who "governs him while obeying him," which is how Rousseau wants his tutor to govern Emile. (p. 371) Rousseau is in no doubt that her "proper purpose" in society is to bear children, maintain the family's unity and stability, and sustain her husband. (p. 362) Hence her infidelity is many times more pernicious than a man's because it "dissolves the family and breaks all the bonds of nature" causing untold social and political disorder. (p. 361) This is what Sophie learns as she is educated to be a wife and mother.

Because her looks are so important for her a girl's *amour-propre*, or vanity, unlike a boy's, must not be discouraged – it is also what gives her mother power over her. Because she will need strength to bear children she must exercise hard, though differently from a man. Because "everything that hinders and constrains nature is in bad taste," she must learn to act and dress naturally. (p. 367) She must learn to make clothes for her dolls in preparation for her future role as a mother. The principles of utility and readiness apply to her education as much as they do to Emile's. She must learn to read, to write, to do arithmetic, but only to the degree that will be useful for her. Her natural intelligence is more precocious than a boy's, and because a woman's life "is a perpetual combat against herself," she must learn to "conquer herself" earlier than he does. (p. 369) Hence her mother's discipline must be strict, preparing her for the "docility" she will need as a woman, since in her life she will "never cease to be subjected either to a man or to the judgments of men." Unless he is "a monster" her gentleness, her "first and most important quality," will always bring a man "around and triumphs over him sooner or later." (p. 370) She is not, however, to be brutalized by the discipline nor deprived "of gaiety, laughter, noise, and frolicsome games." (p. 370) She must learn "the art of getting looked at," or "the art of coquetry," which she will, however, learn to practice always with due modesty. (p. 373) She will be raised to be lively, to play, dance, sing, and enjoy life in general, speak easily, politely and entertainingly. She will be taken to festivals and ceremonies and will participate in them with good taste.

Unlike Emile's her religious education will be strictly conventional, because, in Rousseau's view already stated in his earlier discussion of taste, she is incapable of abstract reasoning. This is, of course, nonsense, but in his eighteenth century view women's reasoning "is practical and makes them very skilful at finding means for getting to a known end, but not at finding that end itself ... the woman learns from the man what must be seen and the man learns from the woman what must be done." In this reciprocal educative relationship, modelled earlier in the relationship between Wolmar and Julie "each obeys and both are masters." (p. 377) But a woman's reflections, he insists, "ought to be directed to the study of men or to the pleasing kinds of knowledge that have only taste as their aim; for, as regards works of genius, they are out of the reach of women." (p. 386) This view, of course, colours his political view of her limited role as a citizen. On the other hand, while "men will philosophize about the human heart better than she does," (p. 387) she is "the natural judges of men's merits," (p. 390) and "will read in men's hearts better than they do." (p. 387) Hence Rousseau reserves the domain of "experimental morality" to woman, man is more at home with moral concepts and systems. Put more simply, "woman has more wit, man more genius; woman observes, and man reasons." (p. 387) Ideally Rousseau would have her "limited to the labours of her sex alone and left in profound ignorance of all the rest," (p. 382) but this is dangerous "in big cities and among corrupt men," where she needs her wits to protect her virtue. (p. 383)

Sophie is taught the true virtue of chastity not by disparaging her body or by stunting her natural passions but by making her feel the true value of purity so that she comes to love it:

"Depict for them the good man, the man of merit; teach them to recognize him, to love him, and to love him for themselves; prove to them that this man alone can make the women to whom he is attached – wives or beloveds – happy. Lead them to virtue by means of reason. Make them feel that the empire of their sex and all its advantages depend not only on the good conduct and the morals of women but also on those of men, that they have little hold over vile and base souls, and that a man will serve his mistress no better than he serves virtue. You can then be sure that in depicting to them the morals of our own days, you will inspire in them a sincere disgust!" (p. 392)

"This is the spirit in which Sophie has been raised," when Emile finds her. (p. 293) At sixteen she is lovable, pure, attractive though not beautiful, speaks little and listens a lot, is of seemly bearing and decent conversation, and so on. Her religious beliefs are simple and her virtue is "her dominant passion ... Sophie," the author of *Emile* declares, "will be chaste and decent until her last breath" – like Julie – fateful words, as we shall see. (p. 397) Like Julie she is raised to love and esteem her parents and to bow to their judgment. At fifteen her father has already spoken to her of marriage, "for the destiny of life depends on marriage, and there is never too much time to think about it." (p. 399) Emile discovers her by chance at her parents' house where he and his tutor seek accommodation for the night. She too has sought for the right man long and unsuccessfully. When she accepts Emile (who falls madly in love with her at first sight) as her suitor she takes possession of his soul which he surrenders to her willingly, while he teaches her about the deeper things he has learnt.

This would seem to be the obvious ending to the story but, to Emile's dismay, his education is still incomplete. He must learn "how to conquer his affections" and follow his conscience, to "keep himself in order" in everything so that nothing, not even his love for Sophie, "can make him deviate from it." (pp. 444–445) Two hard years of separation are required, spent travelling with his tutor when he will learn also "to consider himself in his civil relations with his fellow citizens;" i.e. to be a citizen. (p. 455) His curriculum is impressive. He must become "versed in all manner of government, in public morals, and in maxims of state of every kind." (p. 458) This requires him to go "back to the state of nature," and to "examine whether men are born enslaved or free, associated with one another or independent" (for which the *Second Discourse* would be a suitable text-book). (p. 459) He then moves on to matters of domestic governance, sovereignty, the social contract which determines the political relations between peoples and their rulers, the concept of the general will, of democracy and political obligation in general, and so on, all amply discussed in the *Third Discourse* and the *Social Contract*. Then on, to the larger themes of federalism, international relations, just war theory, and the union of the states of Europe, discussed by the Abbe de Saint-Pierre. In short, his tutor would take Rousseau's political writing as the text-books for Emile's education, "a strategy that," not only "reveals the close connection Rousseau saw between the 'principles of political right' of the *Social Contract*, and the educational principles of *Emile*," but also indicates the didactic purpose for which he intended his political writing. (Roosevelt 1990, p. 4)

Emile learns the lesson of the *Discourses*, that the closer men are to nature, "the more their character is dominated by goodness," and that "it is only by closing themselves up in cities and corrupting themselves by means of culture that they become depraved." (1772b:1991, p. 469) He returns from his tour suitbly disillusioned with European politics; there is, he learns, no true liberty there and no safeguard to be found under the laws. True freedom, he concludes, is "found in no form of government; it is in the heart of the free man" who lives "the morality of his actions and the love of virtue." (p. 472–473) Sophie, he decides, is the only chain his heart will bear. He will, however, live in the land of his birth, among his people as a friend and benefactor to them and as a good citizen, despite his dissatisfaction with their laws and habits. He will live "a patriarchal and rustic life, man's first life, which is the most peaceful, the most natural, and the sweetest life for anyone who does not have a corrupt heart." Together with his Sophie he will "vivify the country and reanimate the extinguished zeal of the unfortunate village folk," bringing in a new golden age for them where their fields become more fertile, the countryside beautiful, and where their work is transformed into festivals. The only threat to his happiness, Rousseau reflects grimly, will arise if he takes on "the sad job of telling the truth to men," which he must avoid doing. (p. 474) This is the idyllic future Rousseau contemplates for the newly weds at the end of *Emile*. The tutor's work seems over; he counsels them together on the elements of an enduring marital union. She will keep her husband by "managing your pleasures in order to make them durable." This will give her a hold on him when "the attraction of mutual confidence succeeds the transports of passion" – she will still remain his wife and friend, and the mother of his children, and he will live happily at home with his family. (p. 479) His work complete, the tutor's rest is due, and well-earned. Sophie is soon pregnant; if it is a boy, Emile declares, he will be his son's tutor and mentor and a true father. But he wants *his own* tutor and friend to continue as *his* master; indeed, as "the master of the young masters," to advise and govern the family from a distance for ever – their Legislator. (p. 480) The book ends on this idyllic note.

SUMMARY AND COMMENT

As we have seen, *Heloise* and *Emile* are very different 'novels'. *Heloise* showcases an ideal domestic education with a patriarchal structure and wife and husband who play complementary roles in the governance-education of their household, and not just of their children but also of the servants. The education is informal, lived rather than formally instructed as in the public schools. The same education as the citizens in the *Social Contract* on the larger, but still intimate, scale of the city-state. *Heloise* also anticipates many of the key views about the education of children found in *Emile* which Julie puts into practice until the boys are of an age when they are turned over to a male tutor and tested friend, St Preux. With *Emile*, Rousseau takes a step back; in the absence of contemporary households like the Wolmars' he wants to show us how a Wolmar and a Julie capable of the matrimonial partnership of the Wolmars can be educated. Emile's, a boy's, education takes the same course as the natural evolution of man from a solitary in the first years, outside any social or domestic influence and entirely in the hands of a tutor who, like St Preux, is a trusted family friend, to a fully self-fulfilled married man, father, and citizen. A girl's education, left unmentioned in *Heloise* despite the presence of Henriette, except for the comment that, unlike the boys', it will continue to be her mother's responsibility, is also taken up exhaustively in *Emile*. In the book Sophie is educated in a domestic setting, contrary to Emile. The object is to educate the two differently according to their gender but into the harmonious complementarity of the Wolmars. The suggestion is that they will eventually create a strong family like the Wolmar together which will be the first building block for the ideal society of the *Social Contract*.

As I remarked in the previous section, Rousseau has been consistently criticised, often unfairly, for his views on women and their education. Gauthier identifies "a contradiction" at the heart of *Emile* in that Sophie "is human but she is not born to be free;" (2006, p. 42) her life is pre-defined entirely in terms of the service she gives a man and her family. She is denied the individuality Rousseau prizes in Emile who is educated, as a man at least, as an autonomous being – at least apparently. William Boyd rightly dismisses Rousseau's justification of his different treatment of the sexes, that he was simply following 'nature'. "Here plainly," Boyd remarks, "'nature' speaks the language of eighteenth century prejudice." (1968, p. 117) But "prejudice" is not completely inexcusable and one must not forget, in Rousseau's defence, that the appeal to "nature" had an ancient currency in his time and was a perfectly valid tool of philosophical thought shared by many. Locke, before him, had assumed that the patriarchal model of the family was endorsed by the Bible, and had shown the same prejudice against women also putting them in a subservient role to men. (Spring 1994, p. 115) Rousseau himself believed that his optimistic view of nature could be justified theologically against Hobbes his materialist predecessor, and that the model of the patriarchal family structure could also be justified biologically and anthropologically, by going back to the very first human association, the nuclear family.

Readings of Rousseau as a misogynist fearful of women and wishing their subjugation because of his personal sexual inadequacies and unhappy experiences with them, narrated with varying degrees of honesty in the *Confessions*, fail to square with his treatment of Julie the protagonist of *Heloise* and, as I remarked earlier, far from a powerless accommodating woman, and the spirited Sophie we see before she marries Emile. As Strong puts it, the "major thrust" of Book Five of *Emile* is not the subjugation of women but "to establish that not only is the woman's place in the home but the home is that which can make men want to be virtuous citizens." (2002, p. 134) This, making men virtuous citizens, is the all-important educational role Rousseau sees women as fulfilling with respect to their husbands and male children. Already announced in his letter to the citizens of Geneva preceding the *Second Discourse*, it coincides with his general views on the political education of citizens discussed in the last section of Chapter One above. "Amiable and virtuous women citizens," he says, "it will always be the fate of your sex to govern ours. Happy it is when your chaste power, exercised only within the conjugal union, makes itself felt *only for the glory of the state and the public happiness*." (1755a:1987, p. 31, italics added) Strong continues to describe Rousseau as "one might say, sexist, but, in contemporary jargon, not phallocentric," and this, I think, is a good assessment of this side of his work. (2002, p. 136) On the evidence of *Heloise* he wanted women to be active and happy wives and responsible mothers, operating under the invisible jurisdiction of their husbands, the domestic equivalent of the Founder-Legislator. Julie is the mistress of the house, the visible power who manages the household and raises the children, Wolmar makes the principles, the constitution, with which she manages it.

QUESTIONS FOR CHAPTER TWO

1. Critically discuss the role Rousseau gives to domestic education in society and his conclusions about the kind of family he believed could carry out this role successfully. Do you think his views on the subject are still relevant today?
2. Friendly commentators contend that reading *Emile* is still a valuable experience for teachers today. Would you agree? If not, why? If yes, which are the aspects of Rousseau's educational philosophy in the book that you think still relevant for teachers?
3. Using Rousseau's work on the subjects comment critically on any of the following:
   (a) education for solitude
   (b) education as governance
   (c) education as self-mastery
   (d) self-education

CHAPTER 3

ROUSSEAU IN PERSPECTIVE

AFTERMATH OF *EMILE* AND CONCLUDING YEARS: 1762–1778

Fleeing arrest in Paris any illusion Rousseau may have entertained of returning home to Geneva was quickly dashed. *Emile* was burnt in the city and a warrant issued for his arrest on 18th June. The *Social Contract* was banned in France. There was agitation against him in Berne and Neuchatel when he moved to these cities, and as the intolerance grew he became a homeless fugitive, denounced by clerical edicts and pursued by mobs, insulted and chased in the streets "as if I were a were-wolf." (1770:1953, p. 579) The edicts were the signal for an outcry "against me throughout Europe, a cry of unparalleled fury," which was not to abate for years. (p. 545) Settling in Motiers in July 1762 after a short respite in Yverdon, he writes of having "completely given up literature" and seeking a quiet retirement. (p. 555) In March of 1763 he renounced his Genevan citizenship and wrote the *Letter to Christophe de Beaumont* in reply to the archbishop's edict against him. In autumn of that year Jean-Robert Tronchin, Public Prosecutor of Geneva, a conservative and an old enemy, published *Letters Written from the Country*, defending the actions taken against him by the republic. He replied in December 1764 with his *Letters Written from the Mountain* which instigated an "appalling outburst" against him. (p. 575) Earlier that year, in August, an M. Buttafoco, a leading Corsican patriot, commissioned him to write the *Project for a Constitution for Corsica* which he left unfinished at his death and which was only published in 1861.

Meanwhile, obsessed with saving his reputation from books and articles circulating falsely under his name or under pseudonyms attributed to him, we find him projecting a definitive authorised edition of his full works. By the year 1765, near to completing his *Dictionary of Music*, he described himself "A tortured creature, battered by every kind of storm, and wearied by many years of travelling and persecution." (p. 600) That same year his house in Motiers was stoned by a mob. Driven from the town, he retreated to the small tranquil island of St Pierre in the middle of Lake Bienne which he had once visited with a friend, wanting "no more traffic with mortal men," seeking to be left alone with Therese and his botany which had grown into a passion over the years. This was not, however, to be. His respite was again brief. Barely two months later he was expelled from the island and from all the Bernese territories by the authorities, and warned never to return. These developments completely ruined his plan to write the Corsican constitution that winter.

Returning to Paris again, he was forced into exile in England in January 1766, a country he disliked, where he was hosted by the Scottish philosopher David Hume. At Hume's home at Wotton he worked hard on the *Confessions*. His paranoia, however, had grown ever stronger with his experiences. Quarrelling bitterly with Hume he was back in France in May of 1767 wandering from place to place in search for a safe haven, often using false names to protect himself. In November of that year he finally published his *Dictionary of Music*. In August of 1768, now aged fifty-six, he married Therese in Bourgoin. In 1770, back in Paris yet again, he finally finished the *Confessions*. He read from them to friends but the work remained unpublished at his death. In 1771, a Count Wielhorski commissioned him to write *Poland*, which also remained unpublished in his lifetime though copies of the manuscript circulated widely when it was finished. In 1772, in a state of extreme mental agitation, he began writing the *Dialogues* which he completed in 1776, and finished *Elementary Letters on Botany*. Both these works were also unpublished at his death. He tried unsuccessfully to place the manuscript of the *Dialogues* on the high altar of Notre Dame Cathedral in Paris on February 24 of that same year. His obsession with persecution had now reached an acute point and the *Dialogues* were quickly followed by a self-justificatory pamphlet addressed *To all Frenchmen who still love justice and truth*, which he distributed by hand and which was also published posthumously. That same year he was involved in a serious but fortuitous accident that may have ultimately cost him his life. Returning home from a walk in the outskirts of Paris he was knocked down by a Great Dane, suffering severe concussion and several head injuries in the process. He describes the incident in the 'Second Walk' of the *Reveries*, his last work which he also began writing in 1776, and in which he made his last entry, dated, Palm Sunday 1778. He died shortly afterwards at Ermenonville on May 20th.

The *Reveries* contains "passages of ecstasy and tranquillity," and, "taken as a whole, is more serene than the preceding *Dialogues*." But the "obsessions with enemies and extravagant protestations of innocence," remain the same, and the work also "breathes self-doubt, self-pity and self-aggrandizement." (France 1979, p. 14) The volumes of *Collected Works* Rousseau had projected were published not long after his death between 1780 and 1789, and included several unpublished pieces. The personal vindication he had thirsted for and never came in his lifetime, arrived not long after in 1794, not, ironically, from his beloved native city of Geneva but from the French nation, when the Revolutionary government moved his body from the Ile des Peupliers where it was buried to its final resting place in the Pantheon in Paris, the place of heroes.

REACTIONS TO *EMILE*

Not all the immediate reactions to *Emile* when it was published were of condemnation and criticism. A host of contemporaries at home and abroad read Rousseau's book with admiration and passionately defended its contents against its critics and detractors. Not very long after his death forward-looking educators, like the Swiss Pestalozzi, and the Germans Basedow, (1724–90), Herbart (1776–1841), and Froebel (1782–1852), drew on its contents for the innovative teaching approaches they explored in their settings. It was soon translated in London, twice over, and became famous and influential in Germany where it was acclaimed by such thinkers as Kant, Lessing, Goethe, and Herder. Bernadette Baker observes a dearth of new publications for well over a century between 1763 and 1883, but this, she remarks, "does not mean the non-circulation of the ideas that had been espoused." (2001, p. 16) Indeed, towards the close of the nineteenth century the book's influence on education in Europe and the United States, grew apace. A 'new' movement began to "focus on *Emile* for its techniques," and this led to "its canonization in Educational literature by the turn of the twentieth century." (p. 1) It proclaimed "the *Rights of Childhood*" throughout Europe, Federika Macdonald, writing in 1906, declared, just as the *Social Contract* had earlier proclaimed the 'rights of man'. It "laid the foundation for our new theory of education, and taught the civilised world remorse and shame for the needless suffering and the quenched joy that throughout long ages had darkened the dawn of childhood." (Rusk 1979, p. 115) Compayre, writing at about the same time, similarly describes it as "the charter of childhood's freedom." (1908:2002, p. 24) Macdonald speaks of "harsh systems, founded on the old medieval doctrine of innate depravity," being "overthrown" by its influence, (Rusk 1979, p. 115) And Baker points out that *Emile* was a standard text in teacher education right across the United States in the late nineteenth century "insofar as it was deemed necessary to the historical study of pedagogical techniques." (2001, p. 1)

The widespread enthusiasm for Rousseau's ideas continued through the first half of the twentieth century thanks to the influence of the 'progressive movement' in education, about which more will be said below. Today, when the enthusiasm is gone, *Emile* is still recognised as the beginning "of pedagogical reflection on childhood," and "still seems to be able to lay claim to relevance for issues of pre-school education kindergarten or family pedagogy." (Peukert 1999, pp. 215–216) But Rousseau's direct influence on research and policy documents is minimal, to say the least. (p. 216) Moreover, his critics remain among scholars who occasionally take up his work. Jurgen Oelkers, has recently criticised *Emile* as a bad novel, as being really only "a long theoretical defence and justification disguised as a novel that ignored the basic rules of novel writing." (2002, p. 690) This may be true or not. In either case, it is not an aspect of *Emile* that interests us here. More relevant to the scope of this last chapter is Oelkers' comprehensive denial of a number of claims about Rousseau and his influence on modern education that have grown customary over the years. One such claim is this one that *Emile* marked the beginning of a new or modern thinking about education in the late nineteenth-early twentieth century I am referring to. Oelkers bestows this honour on Jean Piaget instead.

Oelkers claims that *Emile*'s pedagogy is not based on a psychology of human development like Piaget's, it therefore lacks a fundamental feature of this thinking. What Rousseau's book draws on instead is "a theory of solitude." (p. 688) This is a reading of *Emile* that first appeared in Jean Starobinski's famous and influential work *Jean-Jacques Rousseau: Transparency and Obstruction*, in 1971 and which I shall remark on a bit more later. Piaget was the director of the *Rousseau Institute* in Geneva in 1921 and his first influential article on education appeared in the *Encyclopedie Francaise* in 1939, nearly two centuries after *Emile* was published. Oelkers also contests the description of Rousseau as 'modern', a 'modernist' ahead of his times, as he has sometimes been described. Laying aside the well-known ambiguity of the concept of the modern and what it designates, which he rightly remarks about, he argues that Rousseau himself decried everything considered modern in his day, not excluding what were regarded as the more advanced or 'scientific' ways of learning, and distanced himself from them. Oelkers denies that this means that he was a "true conservative" either, as others have characterised him. While Rousseau regarded any kind of pedagogy that sacrifices the present for the future as 'barbaric', he remarks, he rejected the idea that it has to do with the past with equal vigour. (p. 682) His pedagogy was, Oelkers concludes, entirely concerned with the present – but this is surely one way, at least, of connecting it with new or modern thinking, with progressivism. So what can one make of these claims of Oelkers?

RELATION WITH MODERNITY

Rousseau himself, as we saw, claimed for the pedagogy of *Emile* that it constitutes the visionary, though not impossible, dreams of a revolutionary. Indeed, his first injunction to the Tutor is to disregard contemporary opinions and to do the contrary of what is being done? But was he being honest? Did *he* disregard contemporary views to do the contrary? The evidence of the *Confessions* shows the growth of a mind which steeped itself in the theories and ideas of the contemporary and earlier philosophers and thinkers, of Plato, Hobbes, Locke, Descartes, Montaigne, Spinoza, the Port Royal thinkers, the contemporary *philosophes*, and so on, and in Classical literature also. But it is a mind finally determined to go its own way like the man who owned it when he symbolically changed his outward appearance and openly became a new man, a 'foreigner' in his society, like Emile. However, it did not grow in a wilderness of ideas about education as he complained either. To the contrary the period was rich in writings on the subject following the success of Locke's treatise.

Michel Soetard remarks a new interest in children at the time which was not restricted to him, that "The books, sections of books and articles" on the subject were "literally legion." (1994, p. 423) In 1758, a very few years before *Emile* appeared, Helvetius wrote *Of the Mind* which already claimed education to be the key to everything in life, the Abbe de Saint-Pierre had published a *Project to Improve Education*, and La Chalotais an *Essay on National Education*. Saint-Pierre had also discussed the idea that men and women should be educated separately. (Gilead 2005) Other notable predecessors and contemporaries who wrote about education in 1758 also, were Fenelon and Condillac. The first's *Treatise on the Education of Girls* (1689) Rousseau almost certainly knew. Other works by lesser known thinkers, like Fleury's *Treatise on Study Choices and Method* were popular enough to be published more than once (twice in his case, in 1753 and 1759) within a short period of time. Another work, Rollin's thoughts on education in his *Treatise on Studies*, heralded Rousseau's thinking in many ways, and though Rousseau seems not to have known of his work, Turgot had already criticised contemporary education for being contrary to nature, and condemned the practice of filling children's heads with abstract notions that they could not be expected to grasp, ten years before *Emile* appeared. Turgot had also anticipated Rousseau's view, echoed by romantic pedagogy since, that "'All the virtues have been sown by nature in the heart of man: the one thing needful is to let them blossom forth'." (Compayre 1908:2002, p. 9)

Scholars are divided on the extent, if any, to which he may have borrowed from these writings. (Soetard 1994) It seems improbable that he knew none of them at all. But even if he knew them all Rousseau's unique genius is the writing of *Emile* as a whole, which still reads as a revolutionary work today in its basic pedagogical theses, never mind its style – which falls somewhere indeterminately between a novel and a treatise. In any case, if he did draw on their ideas, this would contradict Oelkers' claim that he was out of sympathy with the advanced thinking of his time which they represented, and if he didn't it would still show that he was in tune in spirit, at least, with what the most advanced contemporary thinkers on education of the time were saying. So let's turn to the thesis that he was anti-modern. It certainly finds support from the fact that he declared open war on the contemporary bourgeois vision of Western civilized progress of his time articulated by the *philosophes* from his very first *Discourses*. There is also no mistaking his explicitly stated preference for ancient societies and peoples like the Spartan, Roman, and early Christian to the contemporary societies of Europe (especially the nation states), and for literary Classics over contemporary writing of all kinds which he dismissed with enormous disdain. By distancing himself from the status quo's most radical critics, the *philosophes*, he disqualified himself from being counted among the progressive thinkers of his time as they were then considered. On the other hand, he did not subscribe to the conservative's nostalgia for a return to some real or mythical ideal socio-political order in the past of which the present would be a degeneration. His point of reference, his return, was to nature instead; to a time, an order, before time, *beyond* the past, beyond history, to a hypothetical pre-social beginning. And this marks him as a radical of a different kind, a romantic rebel in today's terminology, a revolutionary.

Having done his best to demolish the credentials of the present dispensation, of the *status quo*, *philosophes* and all, we find him returning to the drawing board to start again in education and politics, from the very beginning, from 'man' himself, with the writing of *Emile, Heloise,* and the *Social Contract,* revolutionary works capable of attracting the admiration of such as Pestalozzi, Froebel, Dewey, Makarenko, and Freinet, all revolutionary thinkers and educators in their right. On the other hand, this same revolutionary thinker, paradoxical and contradictory at every turn if nothing else (and therefore certainly modern in this sense), was capable, as we saw, of the conservative nationalism of *Poland* where we find him attacking the modernizers and reformers among the Polish people and describing the 'modernist' trends in the rest of Europe of his time as "hastening [it] to its doom." But does his anti-modernism, i.e. his dislike for the Enlightenment thinking of his day, disqualify him from being modern?

There is another way, more relevant for us, of judging the matter of his modernity than in terms of his sympathies and declarations, this is by seeing if his thought can be located in the modern world. In this respect Strong refers to him as "the first modern (Westerner)" because his "work impresses upon his readers", he says, the "problems and inadequacies of that which passes for human society," and "does so by raising the question of what a human society *is*," which, in its reflexivity, is an entirely modern question. (2002, p. xxiii, italics in original) Strong claims even more strongly that "What we mean by modern can be seen by looking at Rousseau," and if he "is not the whole story of modernity," he is, "in ways that others around him were not, *modern*." (p. 3, italics in original) In other words, Rousseau captures the spirit of the modern in his person, in the way he experienced the world he lived in, its tensions and contradictions which were reflected in his own person and in his writing. Also in his sense of being radically at odds with his society, a stranger, of an authentic self within struggling to find its true voice in an alien world, later articulated in romanticism and its off-shoots, which gives rise to the central project of *Emile* "to develop a person who does not live in contradiction with himself," which is what being well-ordered means. (Blits 1991, p. 404)

Finally, Rousseau is distinctly modern in his very critique of the emerging bourgeois society of his time, of its psychology, its political culture and its moral climate, the existence at its very heart of the deep-rooted condition of an alienated humanity. This characterisation of the alienated state of human being in the modern bourgeois world (incorporating his critique of private property and analysis of the roots of social and political inequality in the *Second Discourse*), not so much through "a philosophical or sociological theory of alienation," as "a phenomenological description of social man's alienated condition," anticipates Hegel, Marx, and a line of critical social theory that followed. (Inston 2006, p. 349)

EDUCATION FOR SOLITUDE

Is *Emile* a 'theory of solitude', as Oelkers characterizes it, and was solitude Rousseau's "only real obsession (Starobinski 1971)," as he quotes from Starobinski? (2002, p. 686) This is Rousseau's own pertinent response to the question: "If writings emerge from the hands of such a solitary, they will surely resemble neither *Emile* nor *Heloise*." (1776a:1990, p. 149) Certainly the education for solitary self-sufficiency which *was* the object of the first phase of Emile's education was not the complete project. Describing Emile's education as intended for the life of a solitary fails to square with the fact that in the book his education into manhood is completed only with his relationship with a woman and at her hands, and at the point when it bears fruit and he becomes a husband and a father. Besides, Emile is also taken abroad to receive his final preparation for his life among 'men', in his society and as a member of the wider, more cosmopolitan European world, which his tutor would hardly have bothered with were Emile intended for a solitary life.

But *was* Rousseau himself obsessed with solitude? Such an obsession can be of different kinds; one can love and welcome it or fear and loathe it. Rousseau seems to have experienced both; he certainly prized his solitude, his leisurely solitary excursions and aimless wanderings in the countryside and the hours he spent alone in his study that were so crucial to his writing and thinking, but he also feared it in the shape of his enforced rejection by his fellow-men. In the *Reveries* he writes of his delight on the island of St Pierre with being alone with his botanical studies, but he also describes himself as "the most sociable and loving of men," and complains bitterly about having been "cast out by all the rest." (1776b:1979, p. 27) In *Emile*, as we saw, he described solitary man in his primitive state, despite his happiness and peace, as "stupid and unimaginative," his advance into a social state as a net gain, a "happy moment" whereby he became an "intelligent being." In short, 'man', in Rousseau's conception of things, is *both* a creature of solitude which he enjoys, and one of conviviality, which he requires for his self-fulfilment, and he himself prized both these aspects of being in his life. The educative and political value he attached to conviviality is evident, to repeat, in the repeated emphasis he made on the fraternal potential of activities that bring people together amicably for different purposes; festivals, games, feasts, ceremonies, and so on, which he celebrates and recommends in all his writings from the *Second Discourse* on.

The 'destructive' critique of the first two *Discourses*, which, as I remarked earlier, usually provokes the "regrettably common" view that he was anti-social and yearned for or advocated a return to nature, to solitary man, (Kontio 2003, p. 8) cannot, as Rousseau himself pointed out, be read apart from the constructive writing of *Emile, Heloise,* and the *Social Contract.* Together they promise a new beginning that could achieve authentic progress for humankind. As Gauthier put it, although in the *Discourses* he sought to show "that contemporary Western society alienates the individual from his true nature," he wrote *Emile* and the *Social Contract* "to seek a way to restore man to himself," and it clearly wasn't by returning him to the solitude of his pre-social ancestor. (2006, p. xi) If, in Rousseau's view, "going back to nature," means "abandoning culture" or social life and returning to the solitary existence of the first primitive, then it "means denying humanity itself." (Kontio 2003, p. 8) As we saw, *amour de soi*, the sentiment that dominates the life of pre-social man is only *one* natural sentiment, the other, pity, turns the human being, equally *naturally*, social. "One must not," Rousseau warns us in *Emile*, "confound what is natural in the savage state with what is natural in the civil state;" i.e. there are standards of what is 'natural' in civil society also – the standards he sought to outline in the *Social Contract.* (1762b:1991, p. 406)

This is not to say that there is not a lot to criticise in Emile's first-stage education as a solitary. For one thing, pure self-sufficiency is impossible, nor can his tutor fully replicate the condition of self-sufficiency from which human being began because that would require him to dispense with himself. Children always need grown-ups to provide the basic material and mental conditions of life in their early years of dependence on them; food, clothing, shelter, sympathy and other human reactions, etc. Without these they could not survive. Even the hypothetical solitary primitive must have had a mother if 'he' didn't know his father. In fact, Emile is weaned by a nurse as a baby before he is passed on to his tutor and is subsequently raised in a home, albeit a secluded one, not in a cave in the middle of nowhere. So he will certainly meet with other people besides his tutor as he grows up; servants and other acquaintances made inside or outside the home, and more casual ones in the country lanes or the village streets. These people, however, are invisible in *Emile*, Rousseau brackets them out of his narrative, except for isolated incidents like the one with Robert the gardener. Nowhere else does he describe Emile's interaction with the servants as he does with the Wolmar children in *Heloise*. How is Emile encouraged to regard them? Not as inanimate props on the stage of his upbringing surely! If for no other reason, because it would be counter-productive later when his tutor wants him to cross over into social life and to develop a humane, fraternal, attitude towards others. On the other hand, to raise a child as a solitary in a household with servants and their families necessarily requires rendering its members anonymous for him and his relationship with them formal to the degree of being mechanical.

Again, Emile will meet with other children, possibly in the house, presumably in the country-lanes or woods around it – it is inconceivable that he will never see another child while he is growing up! Rousseau is clear, however, that other children must not influence his life; he will not play with them nor be their friend. But to raise him in an entirely childless world is to ensure that *he* is never a child and is surely the recipe to educate not a man but a monster (as Rousseau himself, he believed, was referred to in his society). Several times he concedes that a monster is how Emile *will* be regarded by others. Yet his childhood is precisely what the tutor is supposed to value and respect, nay to celebrate! Rousseau replies to this criticism that the critics are wrong because his point of reference is nature not convention and nature is always right, and that it is really children who are raised conventionally who are monsters. But this thinking, based on the more than dubious premise that the natural is the measure of the good or the right, is a recipe for disaster, as his own life should have told him. If children are raised as solitaries they will grow not into 'likeable foreigners' but into monsters incapable of any sort of personal relationship with others, not even with a Sophie.

Another justified complaint is against the delay in Emile's intellectual and moral education, and the controversial ban on books until the age of twelve. The latter is particularly odd given Rousseau's own proclivity towards books and the importance they had for him in his life which he narrates very amply in the *Confessions*. Of course, in eliminating reading from Emile's early education he was inconsistent with the education he received from his own father, but he was perfectly consistent with the demands of a negative education for self-sufficiency which was his own doctrine. But the suggestion that a boy should not read a single book until the age of twelve strikes us as inconceivable madness today. Also going by today's wisdom, an education based on the prevention of evil up to the age of fifteen is no moral preparation for a child at all, even in the impossible conditions of Emile's education. Both intellectual and moral education must begin in the earliest years of life; as they inevitably do when they occur in a conventional domestic environment where children are usually born and live. Of course, this criticism applies only for Emile, Sophie's education coincides immediately with her socialisation into her role as a woman and mother. Nor does it apply for the Wolmar boys, which occurs in a conventional domestic setting, differently from a girl's but at the hands of their mother before they are passed on to their male tutor. It is clear from Rousseau's writing that this, the domestic sort rather than as a solitary, is the kind of education he thought preferable for a boy, were there domestic settings like the Wolmar's around that could be trusted with the task – the whole object of *Emile* was to create such a setting for their children with Emile and Sophie.

I have commented quite a bit already in the previous chapter on Sophie's education and Rousseau's views on women. Thirty years after he published *Emile*

Mary Wollstonecraft wrote *A Vindication of the Rights of Women* (1792) with Emile in mind where despite sharing many of his assumptions about human being and society, and about the centrality of the family in preserving the moral fabric of society and the undermining influence of 'vanity' on it, she was critical of these views and argued for coeducation, and for egalitarian schooling. She rightly attributed sexual difference and the role vanity plays in women's lives not to nature but "to the crippling conventions of socialization," and this was the beginning of a feminist revolt against the contents of *Emile*. (Donald 1992, p. 10) But not all feminist judgments on Rousseau are negative. Jane Roland Martin has praised him as "one of the few truly significant philosophers who have discussed the education of women," defending him against critics who "have not even considered her important enough to be discussed at all." (1981, p. 359)

The controversial way he put the notion of nature to work in his account of the status and education of women in *Emile* is only an aspect of the more general controversy over the way he uses it in general. As we saw, his mention of nature ran into immediate criticism in the *First Discourse* as he was charged with wanting to undo everything civilization had achieved for Western society and to return it to a savage state. This was a view which, as we saw, he distanced himself from at his earliest opportunity. Subsequently the charge more usually made against him is that he puts nature to contradictory and inconsistent uses rendering its meaning incoherent. But, though it is true that he does not limit the word to one consistent meaning this is not to say that he is incoherent. Rusk (1979) identified at least four different uses to which he puts it in *Emile* alone where, he says: (1) it refers to the spontaneous development of the innate dispositions of a child, and is associated with a non-interventionist pedagogy, or the idea of negative education; (2) it is opposed to the man-made, and associated with a preventive pedagogy that eliminates all social influences on Emile before he crosses into the social world; (3) it is identical with simplicity, plainness, and modesty and suchlike moral and social virtues, and contrasted with artificiality, luxury, and vanity, all of them vices; and (4) it is identical with the instinctual and primitive, which are represented as honest and good as against the reflective and sophisticated which are represented as dishonest and depraved.

These are not, however, contradictory or inconsistent uses but complex ways of using the same term in different contexts of meaning. It is neither necessary nor usual for a word to carry one constant meaning whenever it is used, provided that the different uses are clearly signalled by the context. One could, with a different purpose in mind, reduce the complexity of Rousseau's use of the word 'nature' just described by following Reisert and reducing it to a more basic two-fold distinction "between what is 'conformable to nature' or natural relative to some condition," i.e. where the natural is a final standard of human behaviour, of what is good, right, normal etc., "and what is simply or unconditionally natural (because it is a constitutive and permanent component of human nature)," i.e. where natural simply means human, or inherent to the condition of being human. (2003, p. 21) Both usages of the term still, in fact, survive today with the term 'human' used more often than 'natural', and the unnatural described as the inhuman. There is no doubting the rhetorical effect he intended for his claim when Rousseau used it politically to identify man's original condition of freedom and equality as the natural or true condition of humanity, even if it is largely lost on today's reader. The force of his political and educational programme came, as we saw, from his claim that contemporary society distorted the original meaning of these terms, freedom and equality, and alienated its members from their natural condition.

FREEDOM AND GOVERNANCE

The sincerity of Rousseau's commitment to freedom is not itself, I believe, to be seriously doubted. But his actual politics of freedom and its relation to education or governance is another matter, as my concluding section to Chapter One indicated. In one place in *Emile* Rousseau declares that "the first of all goods is not authority but freedom," and describes this as "my fundamental maxim. It needs only to be applied to childhood for all the rules of education to flow from it." (1762b:1991, p. 83) But then he defines the scope of education as docile governance, and this is what, at the bottom, the pedagogy of *Emile* is about. The boy is to be educated into a docile man, husband, citizen. True, he must learn to be free first, but Rousseau's free self is the self-governing self, one whose self-mastery is consistent with his sense of identity, of being one with a collective; a family, society, state whose common good he internalizes – this 'being one' is what he means by the practice of virtue. On the other hand, Emile is *not instructed* or disciplined in any away, unlike the children who would attend the public schools he pointedly described as institutions of *instruction*, the implication being that instruction is a pedagogy fit for those already born to be 'slaves' while Emile would learn freely by *discovery* unfettered by books, study regimes, time-tables or targets, or any other form of direction or intervention by an adult.

But this freedom is an illusion because, although his tutor is invited to stay in the background and to appear merely as the boy's 'accomplice' in the early years, the truth is that he is stage-managing the boy the whole time, and when Emile enters his adolescent years he brings his role of 'master' into the open. One recalls Rousseau's injunction that Emile should always think that he is free but should always be doing his tutor's will, and that his tutor should always be in total control of the boy's learning environment in whatever situation. Put in modern language, it is not the case that the tutor has no curriculum for the education of Emile but that the curriculum is hidden from the boy. Emile is not raised in a haphazard self-willed way. To the contrary his tutor plans his education in all its details, patiently but consistently with the changing rhythms of the boy's nature and experience which he studies carefully and manipulates. In short, it is not that the Emile of the early years is ungoverned but that he is governed indirectly and invisibly by his tutor. At the threshold of manhood, he has learnt to be "accountable to himself for his actions," and his "ignorance" has protected him from moral harm. Now older, with his passions growing, he "has to be stopped by his enlightenment." (p. 318) The first step is his self-knowledge. This is when his tutor steps from the shadows:

> "... to present my accounts to him, so to speak; to show him how his time
> and mine have been employed; to disclose to him what he is and what I am,

what I have done, what he has done, what we owe each other, all his moral relations, all the commitments he has contracted and all those that have been contracted with him, what point he has reached in the progress of his faculties, how much of the road he still has to cover, the difficulties he will find there, the means of getting over these difficulties, what I can still help him with, what he alone must now help himself with, and finally, the critical point at which he stands, the new perils which surround him, and all the solid reasons which ought to oblige him to keep an attentive watch over himself before listening to his nascent desires." (p. 318)

The problem is that this revelation is not intended to put him on the path of independence from his tutor, but to change its basis and make the dependence stronger. It must now be Emile who knowingly and willingly puts himself in the hands of his tutor (like the citizen puts himself in the hands of the general will). "As long as he continues freely to open his soul to me and to tell me with pleasure what he feels," his tutor says, "I have nothing to fear." (p. 319) Emile is spoken to ardently and candidly. His tutor honestly disclaims any motive of disinterestedness in his actions: "I shall reveal that I have done it for myself, and he will see in my tender affection the reason for all my care." This honesty, Rousseau believes, startling as it sounds (at least to me), will inflame Emile's "sentiments of friendship, generosity, and gratitude" towards his tutor, who follows with the following still more startling statement: "You are my property, my child, my work. It is from your happiness that I expect my own. If you frustrate my hopes, you are robbing me of twenty years of my life, and you are causing the unhappiness of my old age." (p. 323)

The question was there from the start: Why should someone who is not his father or guardian take such an interest in a boy as to dedicate his life exclusively to his education? Now we have Rousseau's answer; Emile is not the name of a boy but of a project. He is the name of a Tutor's intellectual and moral property. Like a human being with God, he exists for the happiness he brings his creator. The moral blackmail is Julie's father's when he cruelly demanded that she should sacrifice her happiness to his will, to make him happy. Locke comes to mind also; one's property, he tells us, is what one creates for oneself from the raw materials at hand, what one mixes one's sweat with. Emile is his tutor's creature and his proper attitude to his creator will be that, in Rousseau's view, owed to any creator; awe and gratitude. Thus the elements of Rousseau's theology and religious belief surface here also. The analogy of the Tutor with the artist and the architect holds with the Legislator and Paterfamilias also; they too are, like God, creators, and all achieve their happiness from contemplating their work.

The delusion that Emile has been educated for freedom crashes at this point; encouraging him to think of himself as his tutor's 'property' or 'work' is hardly to encourage him to think of himself as free; by definition property has no will of its own, otherwise it would not be such. Rousseau himself confirms this conclusion. "It has taken fifteen years of care to contrive this hold for myself," he says, "He is now sufficiently prepared to be docile." (p. 332) Docility, the willingness to be governed by others (his tutor, his wife, the state), as was pointed out earlier, not independence, is what Emile's education is really about. Emile's response is appropriately docile; he "eagerly put himself in my safekeeping," and begged "me," his tutor, to remain "my friend, my protector, my master!" To protect him from the "enemies … I carry within myself and which betray me … Make me free," Emile begs in desperation, "force me to be my own master and to obey not my senses but my reason." (p. 325) Where have we heard this before? In the *Social Contract*, of course, where the citizen also is forced to be free. The tutor responds to these pleas with "reserve and gravity." The weight of the request and the solemnity of the new compact between them (similar to the informal compact between the Legislator and the polity that creates civil society and the state), is recognised by both as a "harsh yoke," and they seal it with a hearty embrace. (p. 326) The tutor will intervene with his authority sparingly and will never lose Emile's confidence. Thus, he will be open about his own weaknesses and doubts, the failings of his own humanity. "Let him see that you undergo the same struggles which he experiences," and he will, in turn, "learn to conquer himself by your example." (p. 334)

Emile learns self-mastery through the example of his master who he now studies. It is at this point that one recalls Bloom's remarks (quoted in the Introduction) about the "peculiar beauty of the relationship between teacher and student" *Emile* presents us with, and which, for myself, I find far from beautiful. Emile is prepared for docility towards his wife in their marital relationship with a narrative in which pre-marital chastity is presented to him as "connected with health, strength, courage, the virtues, love itself, and all the true goods of man." He will do everything to preserve it before he enters into marriage, "the sweetest of associations" but also "the most inviolable and holy of contracts." (p. 324) One recalls the final scene in the book, described in the previous chapter, when Rousseau has him enter his tutor's room, announces that he is to be a father, declares that he will raise his son himself, and begs his tutor to "remain the master of the young masters," and to "advise us and govern us." His final words are, "As long as I live, I shall need you." (p. 480) Again Rousseau's ideal *ménage a trois* in the making!

In the late autumn, beginning of the winter of 1762, however, not long after he published *Emile*, he began to write a sequel named *Emile and Sophie, or the Solitaries*. In the story, which was left incomplete, the young couple have not a son but a daughter and instead of living in the country as the ending of *Emile* had anticipated, they move to Paris, that den of iniquity. The tutor has moved out of their life for an unspecified reason (the narrative is told by way of two letters he receives from Emile). Their daughter dies and Sophie becomes unfaithful with another man and pregnant by him. Emile leaves her and goes abroad where, after a series of adventures, he is captured by pirates and enslaved and then becomes the trusted advisor of the ruler of Algeria. Apparently Rousseau intended a happy ending to the story with the reconciliation of the two. Though intriguing the manuscript has little intrinsic value. As Dent (2005, p. 121) remarks, it is hard to be sure what his true intent in writing it was and how much it was influenced by his depression with the hostile reception of *Emile* – which was an optimistic book! No doubt the optimism had turned sour on him with his persecution – perhaps the same had happened to his faith in human nature and its ability to be educated in the way of an Emile and a Sophie! Certainly, as Gauthier remarks, it "cruelly reveals the failure of the Tutor's efforts," to educate Emile. (2006. p. 46) On the other hand it could be emphasising the point that without the Tutor, and perhaps of protectors of other kinds also, Paterfamilias, Legislator, and God, human unions are doomed.

INFLUENCES ON PROGRESSIVISM

I want to conclude by showing why Oelkers's view that because the pedagogy of *Emile* lacks a psychology of development it cannot have influenced progressive education (which is what I assume he means by "new methods"), is wrong. Throughout the book Rousseau insists with the Tutor that a child's learning programme must match its unforced, natural, growth, and that he must be constantly alert to the signs of its natural readiness to learn and respond to them appropriately; that he must have "a proper understanding of the child's nature and the way in which this develops." (Darling & Nordenbo 2003, p. 290) In short, *there is* a theory of development in Rousseau though it is not systematic like Piaget's. Indeed, as we saw, the truth is that Piaget's structure of strictly sequential 'natural' developmental stages is anticipated in *Emile*, that "Rousseau's armchair psychology ... strikingly anticipates" Piaget's conclusions. (p. 290) Contrary to what Oelkers says, this implies a debt on Piaget's part towards Rousseau. John Darling and Sven Erik Nordenbo, who I am here quoting, go on to claim, again more conventionally and against Oelkers, and rightly in my view, that *Emile* was "the first of the classics in the history of progressivism," or the 'new', i.e. child-centred, approach to education (p. 290) that "crept" into the late nineteenth century, became "the most dominant feature in the world of education" in the first decades of the twentieth, and was "at a peak up to the 1930s in northern Europe and Scandinavia with Germany as the main bastion," i.e. much before Oelkers takes Piaget to have founded it. (p. 289) They describe the line of progressive thought from Rousseau (possibly even anticipated by Comenius) to Pestalozzi, Froebel, and to Dewey.

In point of fact, however, progressivism, a complex and controversial movement, changed rapidly over time and continued much later. The fact that twentieth century progressivism was not all of one piece renders its relationship with Rousseau, in turn, a complex one. Some writers, distinguishing it from a romantic pedagogical ideology that appeared at the same time under that name, attribute this to Rousseau's actual influence. (Richmond & Cummings, 2004) In an earlier separate article from this one with Nordenbo, Darling identified Rousseau with a radical romanticism that took centre-stage in education in the United States for a while in the 1960s and 1970s, characterised by its "rejection of teacher or adult authority – however enlightened," and critical of both traditionalist and standard progressive outlooks. (1978, p. 161) Its ranks included such as Paul Goodman, John Holt, Herbert Kohl, Jonathan Kozol, Neil Postman, and Charles Weingartner. In the United States, its home, they were referred to as 'neo-progressives.' (Carbone 1985, p. 400) They romanticised the image of the child, charged orthodox progressivism with compromising with the establishment, and rejected teacher and adult authority in general as intrinsically oppressive. (Darling, 1978: p. 161) Darling traced the "essence" of this radicalism to Rousseau's "enjoinder to the tutor in *Emile* to 'Do the opposite of what is usually done and you will almost always be right'." (p. 158) One of the movement's elements, the deschooling movement led by Ivan Illich, described schooling in general as oppressive, hegemonic, and disabling, and wanted to abolish it and professional teaching alike.

Dewey is another matter, Darling and Nordenbo who rightly in my view represent him as "'undoubtedly the most influential educational philosopher of the twentieth century,'" see little direct influence of his thought on European progressivism. (2003:292) In the United States he served as honorary president of the Progressive Education Association founded in 1919. Later, the American 'progressivists' divided into two groups; Child-Centred and Social Reconstructionist. Dewey's influence is usually associated with the second group whose political orientation was influenced by his pragmatic democratic experimentalism, while the first led to neo-progressivism. (Gutek 2004) His own late views on progressive education are found in *Experience and Education* (1938:1970) where he says: "I am not, I hope and believe, in favour of any ends or any methods simply because the name progressive may be applied to them. The basic question concerns the nature of education with no qualifying adjectives prefixed." (Cahn 1970, p. 261)

Another reason why Oelkers questions Rousseau's influence on progressivism is that, as he rightly says, Rousseau rejected generalising 'the child' in the way that child-centred learning implies. While "gender differences in the central notions and metaphors of progressive education are not appropriate," he points out, they were critical for Rousseau who made them consistently in his writing and drew impli-cations from them. It is remarkable, he rightly remarks, that reading Rousseau "did not lead readers up to and including Piaget to doubt the concept of 'child' and 'child-hood'" itself and to acknowledge the gendered nature of learning. (2002, p. 684) Oelkers says that Dewey was the first to connect child-centred education with Rousseau's thinking in *Schools of To-morrow* (1915) where he identified Rousseau with the theory that education "is *a process of natural growth*." The 'growth' meta-phor, Oelkers rightly remarks, though central to the way Dewey defined education, did not, however, feature in Rousseau's thinking at all, though this does not mean that he had no theory of 'natural growth'. (p. 686) Indeed he had, even if he didn't use the expression. The difference is that Dewey regarded growth not as a natural unfolding but as a social process.

Dewey himself identified "the elements of truth" in Rousseau's statements he was prepared to support; "we find that natural development, as an aim, enables him to point the means of correcting many evils in current practices, and to indicate a number of desirable specific aims." Though he acknowledged 'nature' to be "a vague and metaphorical term," he defended its usefulness as a metaphor. For instance, it has inspired us, he says, to the need for a holistic approach to the education of children that considers the body as its object as well as the mind, and leads us to recognise the uniqueness of the child with its own nature, and its own rate and mode of development. It consequently requires teachers "to note the origin, the waxing, and waning, of preferences and interests," and to act with rather than against them. Finally, Rousseau has sensitized us, he continues, to the fact that early childhood education is a distinct area of study, and significantly relevant both for the child's present interests and for its future. (1916:1966, pp. 115–116) Earlier, he excused "Rousseau's passionate assertion of the intrinsic goodness of all natural tendencies," as a strategic "reaction against the prevalent notion of the total depravity of innate human nature," of his times, and describes it as having "had a powerful influence in modifying the attitude towards children's interests," today. (pp. 114–115) On the other hand, he dismisses "the notion of a spontaneous normal development" of the child's instinctive activities uninfluenced by adults, embraced by the romantic progressivists, as "pure mythology," and rightly insists that human learning requires a social medium. (p. 114)

Darling and Nordenbo, remark that *Emile* "is not known to many teachers, or even today to teachers of teachers, however enthusiastic they may be about discovery learning." (2003, p. 294) The amnesia could be due precisely to its ideological connection with the progressivist, child-centred curriculum which came to be criticised on many grounds. The ideological purity of the neo-progressivists, i.e. the religious promotion of discovery learning, or learning from direct experience, only and being told nothing, the over-emphasis on process, all of which can be elicited from *Emile*, meant a lot of waste of time and often of frustration for the children themselves. Child-centredness is also criticised for impeding "any effort on the part of schools to hold children accountable for their learning and achievement," to the detriment of discipline and standards, and because the child "is given freedom to make choices but is still immature to choose wisely." (Dunn 2005, p. 159) Critics critical of child-centred education have wanted parents and teachers to be identified more directly as authority figures in the lives of children, and their teaching to be guided by aims, or end-points, and to have a clear direction. Shaver, who rightly sees *Emile*'s influence behind the progressivist thinking criticised in this way, declares that with child-centred education, it is not clear what the point of this education is, nor how it could possibly be worth the extreme costs it rather notoriously demands." (1990: p. 245) But, behind its excesses, the 'point' of child-centred learning is that the individual needs and qualities of the child not *a priori* targets set by its teachers should be the beginning of its education, that the child should be the key protagonist in its own learning, and that education must be patient and unhurried and not leave the child behind, and these also are ideas that come from *Emile*.

CHAPTER THREE QUESTIONS

(1) Critically discuss Rousseau's view that gender differences count in education; that boys and girls should be educated differently but in a complementary way.

(2) Discuss how Rousseau tries to resolve the tension between the need to educate children to be free, or independent, and docile at the same time. How, in your view, with what kind of approach to pedagogy, if at all, could this tension be overcome?

(3) Do you agree that Rousseau's general thinking in politics/education tends towards totalitarianism? If so, could he have avoided this consequence in some way?

BIBLIOGRAPHICAL ESSAY

An overarching thesis of this book, also following his own wishes, has been that Rousseau's writings, particularly those on politics, society, and education, should be read together as a single project; indeed that these aspects of his work are so closely related as to be one. As I pointed out in the 'Introduction' most of the direct interest in his views on education, whether of writers or educators, has focused on *Emile*. Interest in *Emile* is also shown in the large number of commentaries written not specifically about education but about his political works where its political relevance has been explored. The fascination with his person, paradoxical and polemical even as a stance within the Enlightenment, has also guaranteed a vast amount of scholarship on other different aspects of his thought and life and on his other interests. There is little, however, that has been written about his views on state education in any of these kinds of commentaries, or in other studies of his work, which could mean that his commentators have regarded them as largely unremarkable. This is a mistake because given that, unlike *Emile*, these views on state education are largely uninteresting for educators as such or for pedagogy, they are arguably indispensable to an understanding and evaluation of his politics and of *Emile* itself. They are certainly necessary for any work like this book I have written which has sought to give a brief but comprehensive overview of his work on education in general, not just *Emile*, for the benefit of specialists and non-specialists alike.

I have pointed out what most Rousseau commentators agree upon, whatever their substantive disagreements about his work; that his autobiographical writing serves more than its explicit purpose of self-justification and self-vindication for posterity that he assigned to it, and deserves more than its undoubted merit as a literary genre which he practically invented, and than its intrinsic fascination as an account of a complex and controversial life, mind, and personality. It is doubtless a fascinating and valid account (particularly the *Confessions*) of his self-education and a useful source for understanding his ideas. This means that most books on Rousseau, whatever their subject, deal extensively with his biography. But numerous volumes of Rousseau biographies, several of great merit, have also appeared over time. Simpson (2007) identifies Cranston's reasonably recent three-volume biography, *Jean Jacques: the Early Life and Work of Jean-Jacques Rousseau, 1712–1754* (Chicago, 1991), *The Noble Savage: Jean-Jacques Rousseau, 1754–1762* (Chicago, 1991), and *The Solitary Self: Jean-Jacques Rousseau in Exile and Adversity* (Chicago, 1997) as the best and most detailed. "For a shorter account, by a literary critic rather than a philosopher," he recommends Leopold Damrosch's *Jean-Jacques Rousseau: Restless Genius* (Boston, 2005), which reads Rousseau's texts in relation to his psychology. (p. 140) I agree with both recommendations.

A book that enjoyed a very long life, running into several reprints and republications (later at the hands of James Scotland), and placed Rousseau in the company of the 'great educators', was Rusk's *Doctrines of the Great Educators*, which included an extensive chapter on his ideas. However, it was first published in 1918 and though its repeated reprinting over the years would indicate that interest in the 'great educators' continued well into the early decades of the twentieth century, the voice of that company has dimmed considerably over the past decades, in the English-speaking world of education at least, not the least Rousseau's. Oelkers (2002) has assigned the credit for promoting *Emile*'s canonical status as an education classic to Compayre whose commentary and critique on the book, *Jean-Jacques Rousseau and Education from Nature*, appeared in a slim volume in 1908 anticipating much of what was said about *Emile* later. It is still well worth reading today. The only other twentieth century book written specifically on Rousseau and education (again focusing on *Emile*), in the English-speaking world that I know of is Boyd's famous *The Emile of Jean-Jacques Rousseau* (London 1968). That is not to say that Rousseau has disappeared from the pages of the education literature completely. Indeed, reference to his ideas is practically inevitable in some contexts; when child-centred or progressive education, or kindergarten education, for instance, is the subject. Chapters in books and articles in journals about his work or referring to it have continued to appear over the years. Indeed, the reader will find a number of references to journal articles and chapters in the 'References' section of this book. As I pointed out above, *Emile* in particular has benefitted from the fact that practically any book written about Rousseau on whatever subject must refer to it, even if the book is not specifically about education. This means, in turn, that his educational thinking infiltrates practically every book that deals with his thinking.

In the philosophy of education, the virtual loss of interest in Rousseau has coincided largely with the emergence in the middle of the twentieth century of the school of analytic philosophy, with its liberal politics and near-positivistic strain, as the established paradigm of philosophy of education. Analytic philosophy of education was self-consciously anti-historical in its outlook and practically denied any contemporary relevance to the 'great educators' and to the history of ideas in general in its obsession with language. The decline of its near-hegemonic influence in the field only began in the early 1980s, but it brought little respite for the 'great educators' if any. Rousseau who, as Compayre pointed out, wanted to write "for posterity and the future," did not, for one, make any great come-back. (1908:2002, p. 4) Indeed, the postmodernist influences that became fashionable with the decline of analytic philosophy, as Gerald Gutek has pointed out, were even more inhospitable to doctrines and theories like Rousseau's and the other great educators who "purport to speak in a universal voice for educational goals and purposes," than was analytic philosophy, dismissing their writings collectively as Eurocentric and patriarchal theoretical constructions, and little else. (2004, p. 134)

Matters are different where general and introductory commentaries on his work are concerned. One such recent book, notable for its comprehensive over-view of the different facets of Rousseau's life, thinking, and work is Dent's *Rousseau* (Oxford/ New York, 2005). Dent's book "aims to present and assess in a clear and accessible way the arguments and ideas" that are "central to Rousseau's achievement," and to his influence on our times. (p. 2) It is, in a sense, an elaboration of *A Rousseau Dictionary* which he published earlier (1992), and which "covers all of Rousseau's work in a dictionary format." (p. 7) An earlier work which also serves, more or less, the same scope as Dent's book, is Robert Wokler's *Rousseau: A Very Short*

Introduction (Oxford, 2001). Wokler adds reflections on how Rousseau's problems with his contemporary Enlightenment thinking anticipate recent postmodern writing in his work. Timothy O'Hagan's scholarly book *Rousseau* (London, 2003) published in between, in the Routledge 'Arguments of the Philosophers' series, aims to show Rousseau's merits as a serious philosopher in the light of well-known criticisms of his credentials in the Anglo-saxon world. And a slightly more recent introductory work than all these is Simpson's *Rousseau: A Guide for the Perplexed* (London/ New York, 2007), already referred to. Simpson's book narrows its focus by taking up Rousseau's own claim that the three key texts that constitute his principal works were the *First* and *Second Discourse*, and *Emile*, adding also the *Social Contract* because "many philosophers consider it a masterpiece." (p. ix)

Gauthier (2006) who has himself written a fascinating book on Rousseau and freedom, points out that among the books on Rousseau that have attained a weighty reputation with Anglophone readers as serious commentaries on his work, one needs to include Shklar's *Men and Citizens: A Study of Rousseau's Social Theory* (Cambridge, 1969), Starobinski's *Jean-Jacques Rousseau: Transparency and Obstruction* (Chicago, 1971), and Dent's *Rousseau Dictionary* already mentioned. One could add Bloom's influential introductory essay to his translation of *Emile* which has been used in this book for reference purposes. Though Shklar's book is a bit old, it still constitutes one of the most insightful studies into Rousseau's political work, while Starobinski remains an influential point of reference for students of Rousseau of all kinds. The fact that both are presently out of print (the latter in its English version at least) and difficult to obtain outside a good university library, is sad. Starobinski deals with different aspects of the philosopher's life and thought by "analyz(ing) Jean-Jacques's literary creation as if it represented a kind of imaginary action and to analyze his behaviour as if it constituted a lived fiction." (p. xi) Other very good, more recent, studies of Rousseau's overall thinking are Gauthier's *Rousseau: the Sentiment of Existence* (Cambridge, 2006), Reisert's *Jean-Jacques Rousseau: A Friend of Virtue* (Ithaca/London, 2003), and Strong's *Jean-Jacques Rousseau: The Politics of the Ordinary* (New York/Oxford, 2002), all amply quoted from in this book and referred to already. The reader will have noticed that all the material used for this book is written in English or in English translation, and that includes the Rousseau texts. This is a reflection on my limitations rather than on the validity of the extensive scholarly work done on the philosopher in other languages. It need hardly be said that the reading of the Rousseau texts, whether in the original or in translation, is strongly recommend to the reader.

In a very brief introductory book like this one I have had to be very selective with my own bibliographical resources (listed on another page), and economic in my quotations and commentary. Since the focus of the series is on critical thinkers in education Rousseau's thinking about education has been my major preoccupation although, as I pointed out in the Introduction to this book and at the beginning of this essay, there is no way to separate it from his other concerns, the political and social in particular. Rather than write a study on *Emile*, which is what many earlier writers on Rousseau and education have tended to do, I have written about the full range of his educational thought, including his views about public schooling, domestic education, self-education, and citizen education, which are not so well known. This decision evidently conditioned my choice of the relevant Rousseau texts to focus this study on. Apart from *Emile* these were the three *Discourses*, the *Social Contract*, and *Heloise*, all, I repeat, in excellent translations. Others of his writings have been used more occasionally, his various *Letters* and his autobiographical works in particular (the *Confessions*, *Dialogues*, and *Reveries*), when the necessary connections between his writing and his life had to be made.

Finally, edited scholarly commentaries on the various aspects of Rousseau's thinking are many. Patrick Riley's *The Cambridge Companion to Rousseau* (Cambridge, 2001) in the 'Cambridge Companions to Philosophy' series, surveys the full range of Rousseau's thought and activities in politics and education, psychology, anthropology, religion, music, language, and the theatre, while Lynda Lang's *Feminist Interpretations of Jean-Jacques Rousseau* (University Park PA, 2002) in the Pennsylvania University Press 'Re-reading the Canon' series, addresses the thorny subject of Rousseau's gender politics from different perspectives. A related, and in a sense complementary book is Christopher Kelly and Eve Grace's recent *Rousseau on Women, Love, and Family* (Dartmouth, 2009) which is an anthology of Rousseau's published writings on these subjects. Christopher Bertram's *The Routledge Philosophy Guidebook to Rousseau and the Social Contract* (London, 2004), as the title indicates, is a collection of in-depth studies of the *Social Contract*. Most recently, Christie McDonald and Stanley Hoffmann's *Rousseau and Freedom* (Cambridge, 2010) examines Rousseau's approach to freedom in the context of his thought on literature, women, the body, religion, music, the theatre, and the arts.

GLOSSARY

alienation: Became a central concept in Marxian theory (via the influences of Ludwig Feuerbach (1804–72) and Georg-Wilhelm Hegel (1770–1821)) where it became identified as an effect of capitalism and its system of production. Alienation marks a condition whereby the actual conditions of life in society are contrary to man's 'species being' or 'essential humanity' which is 'his' power to be creative. In the Marxian analysis workers in a capitalist system are cogs in a machine, instruments of the productive apparatus, estranged (alienated) from the process of production, from their product, and from their fellow-workers.

amour de soi: Literally 'self-love', one of the two sentiments, together with 'pity', Rousseau identified as natural to 'men'. *Amour de soi* derives from the instinct of self-preservation which men share with all animals. It is not clear that he wanted to extend this sentiment to women. On the other hand, though he described man's self-love as being entirely self-centred in a natural setting, he distinguished it from a self-centred narcissism in a social setting, in the first nuclear family for instance, where care for oneself needs to be redefined also as care for others.

amour-propre: Rousseau describes the features of *amour-propre* in several places in his work; in modern parlance it can be described as inauthenticity; to live not honestly in one's own eyes and in one's own light, but in the eyes of others. *Amour-propre* is not an unnatural quality, to the contrary it is natural *for social man*; the approval of the other is the basis for all human relationships. Rousseau writes about "the natural game of *amour-propre*," which is "to see what one believes and not what one sees," (1776a:1990, p. 64) and describes it as "the principle of all wickedness" (p. 100) and "a useful but dangerous instrument," (p. 221)

analytic philosophy of education: Analytic philosophy is the name for a style of philosophy that came to dominate the English-speaking world of philosophy in the twentieth century. So it was not remarkable that the pioneers who launched the philosophy of education in the middle of the century chose it for their paradigm. Analytic philosophers saw philosophy as a tool for the rigorous analysis of concepts and the validation of arguments and underplayed the importance of the history of ideas. "Those inspiring this phase of philosophy of education's development saw themselves as aiming for a coherent and systematic rationalization of educational beliefs and practices." (Blake et al. 2003, p. 2)

authenticity: To be authentic is to be true to oneself. This minimal definition assumes a way of thinking that distinguishes an *inner* self which is one's true self from an *outer* self which is one's behavioural self and which is constructed by one's experience of living in a society. The distinction is entirely modern. Being authentic means being true to one's inner self, while being inauthentic means living in the opinion of others, which is what Rousseau meant by *amour propre*.

autonomy: In Enlightenment thinking to be autonomous meant to be directed by laws that one makes for oneself. Worked out as a full ethical theory by Immanuel

Kant (1724–1804), influenced by Rousseau, the adjective 'rational' has often been added to it, to read 'rational autonomy', to emphasise Kant's doctrine that the laws that one makes for oneself must conform with the universal laws of human reason. Rational autonomy was identified by liberal analytic philosophers of education as the aim of education, distinguished from socialization and, more importantly, indoctrination.

bourgeois society: In Marxist literature the *bourgeoisie* are a social and economic class defined by its possession of capital, of the means of economic production, and of a particular culture of possession and exploitation. Their beginnings lie in Medieval times with the rise to political influence of the guild masters, merchants, entrepreneurs, and financiers. In Rousseau's France bourgeois society was composed of the wealthier members of the Third Estate (the First and the Second were the Higher Clergy and the Nobility) who sat in the Estates General, or parliamentary assembly. They created salons where the *philosophes* were invited to argue and expound their ideas and show off their brilliance.

Cartesian: Stemming from the philosophy of the influential French philosopher Rene Descartes (1596–1650). The followers of Descartes are referred to as Cartesians, and the elements of thought that relate or refer to his ideas and theories are called the same.

conscience: The word has been variously interpreted and used. For Socrates it was his *daemon* or guardian spirit, an inner voice that gave him negative guidance; indicating what he should *not* do rather than what he should. The English moralist bishop Joseph Butler (1692–1752) distinguished two aspects of conscience: (a) where it performs a cognitive or reflective function as a tool for judgement of persons and actions; and (b) where it is imperative or authoritarian telling us what course of action we must take. Rousseau refers to it as an 'inner voice' of God speaking directly to 'man' which cannot, therefore, in its judgments, be wrong.

developmental psychology: The systematic study of psychological changes human beings go through over their life-span. Some studies take environment factors, particularly social, into account, others regard cognitive development more narrowly. Jean Piaget's (1896–1980) theory, which pioneered the field, divides cognitive development (or how humans acquire knowledge), into four stages: sensorimotor, pre-operational, concrete operational, and formal operational. The theory has been challenged on different grounds since Piaget.

didactic: That which has the purpose of teaching or instructing. The science and art of teaching in general is referred to in some countries as 'didactics', in others as 'pedagogy'. The latter term is used throughout this book.

Dijon Academy: The Dijon Academy of Science and Fine Letters was founded by Hector Bernard Pouffier, Dean of the Parliament of Bourgogne. The October 1749 issue of *Mercure de France* announced the topic of the 1750 competition as whether the restoration of the sciences and the arts contributed to the purification of morals. The prize for the winner was a gold medallion. (Cress 1987, xxi)

equality: An important concept in the work of Rousseau. "... the farther we are removed from equality, the more our natural sentiments are corrupted," he says in *Emile*. (1762b:1991, p. 406) He distinguished two kinds; natural and social, and insisted that though nothing can be legitimately done about natural inequalities (in height, intelligence, etc.), social inequalities, which were originally created with the institution of property, need to be eradicated from society in the name of natural justice – a belief that was followed later by different kinds of socialists and anarchists.

empiricism: A school of thought usually identified with the English philosopher John Locke (1632–1704) but which can be referred further back to Aristotle who was the first to describe the human mind as a tabula rasa (empty slate or tablet). Empiricists hold that all human knowledge comes from experience, or from the senses, and dismiss the rationalist belief that there are 'innate ideas'. Later followers of Locke were George Berkley (1685–1753) and David Hume (1711–76). The support for empiricism among the *philosophes* was wide-spread with Voltaire (1694–1778) its leading voice.

Encyclopaedia: Jointly edited by Denis Diderot (1713–84) and Jean d'Alembert (1717–83) initially, then by Diderot alone, the *Encyclopaedia, or rational dictionary of the sciences, arts and crafts*, is regarded as one of the great monuments of the Enlightenment expressing the spirit of inquiry and revolt of the age in the name of reason. A best seller in its times, printing to around 25,000 copies in 1789 at the time of the French Revolution, its first volume was published in June 1751. After many transitions in style and content and as a political and economic venture it appeared last as the *Encylopedie Methodique* around 1830.

Enlightenment: A loose intellectual movement which grew in many countries of Europe in the eighteenth century. But its prelude was in the seventeenth century which is known as the 'Age of Reason' because of the advances registered in human knowledge (science especially), and education in this period. The 'movement' promoted a scientific and rational approach to the world and criticised the institutions, beliefs, and practices, religious, moral, cultural and political of the time. Its spirit is captured in Immanuel Kant's (1724–1804) seminal essay *An answer to the question: What is Enlightenment?* dated September 1784.

Enlightenment rationalism: In *Meditations* (1641) Rene Descartes (1596–1650) had claimed that reason is the only reliable source of human knowledge. This belief, known as rationalism, goes with a theory of innate ideas, and of knowledge as a matter of turning the eye into the soul. In other words, it goes back to Plato who also held the same view about the relationship of reason with knowledge. Enlightenment rationalism refers to the positions held by the seventeenth-century philosophers Baruch Spinoza (1632–77), Gottfried Wilhelm Leibnitz (1646–1716), and, to a lesser extent Nicolas Malebranche (1638–1715), beside Descartes.

general will: Rousseau's theory of the general will is fundamental to his political philosophy. As an idea it first appears in a systematic form in the *Third Discourse* but received its full expression in the *Social Contract*. Rousseau defined it as "a form of association which defends and protects with all common forces the person and goods of each associate, and by means of which each one, while uniting with all, nevertheless obeys only himself and remains as free as before." (1762a:1987, p. 148)

informal education: Sometimes referred to as education from experience it is the kind which the learner receives unconsciously and through sources which do not involve the direct instruction of a teacher. It may be natural or involve the conscious manipulation of the environment, material, social, or natural, by the teacher for the learner to interact with profitably.

Lazarist: Lazarists were members of the Congregation of the Priests of the Mission, an institute founded by Vincent de Paul in 1624. The name came from the College of St Lazare in Paris which they occupied until 1792.

materialism: Commonly understood as the doctrine that whatever exists is matter, or entirely dependent on matter for its existence. It denies the Cartesian distinction of the human self into mind and matter and leads to a physicalist outlook which identifies the mind with the brain. Early materialists were the Greek natural pre-Socratic philosophers Anaxagoras (c.500–428 BC), Epicurus (341–271 BC), and Democritus (c.460–c.370 BC). In Enlightenment times, Thomas Hobbes (1588–1679) and Pierre Gassandi (1592–1655), then Holbach (1723–89), Denis Diderot (1713–84), and some other minor thinkers were materialists. Karl Marx (1818–83) and Friedrich Engels (1820–95) later created a philosophy of dialectical materialism and a materialist account of history with economics as its basis.

modernity: A complex term with many meanings. Stuart Hall et al. describe it as "that unique form of social life which characterizes modern societies" which began to emerge in the fifteenth century, though the idea of 'the modern' was only given "a decisive formulation in the discourse of the Enlightenment in the eighteenth century." Its historical evolution has since been "long and complex" and shaped by different national and international forces giving rise to economic, social, and political institutions which, in turn, have grown in their complexity. (1992, pp. 2–3)

natural law: An ancient doctrine that was put to a variety of uses in different cultural contexts and at different times, and is contrasted with *positive* law which is man-made. In Western philosophy the notion of a natural law is customarily dated back to Aristotle (384–322 BC). For Thomas Hobbes (1588–1679) natural law was a precept of reason which instigates human beings to love themselves and preserve their own lives at all costs. Rousseau terms this *amour de soi* and adds another impulse, pity, to it as its social counterpart.

natural right: The most important early modern version of the theory was John Locke's (1632–1704) who believed that human beings are naturally rational and (before Rousseau) good. Locke modified the Medieval doctrines of natural law to argue that because individuals are natural beings they have rights that they bring into society and which no other person or collective could deny them. Thomas Hobbes (1588–1679) and Rousseau, in their own ways and both employing the mechanism of the social contract to show how these rights were safeguarded in a political context, followed on similar lines.

negative education: Negative education is education without instruction and without any pre-defined pedagogical goals on the tutor's part, an education of prevention (from exposure to vice, undue precociousness, the misuse of reason, and so on) rather than action – of ensuring the unfolding of the natural capacities rather than forming the learner with a pre-defined programme. Rousseau defines the principle very succinctly in *Emile* when he says that the Tutor is "to govern without precepts and to do all by doing nothing," though this is not quite precise since, in actual fact, the Tutor must be in total control of the experiential environment of the pupil to eliminate any potentially harmful features. (Strong 2002, p. 117) "I cannot repeat too often that good education must always be negative education," Rousseau said, aimed to "choke off the vices before they are born." (1771:1985, p. 21)

pedagogy: The art and science of teaching (see didactic).

perfectibility: Meaning the indefinite human possibility for self-improvement relative to other human beings and to nature, Rousseau was the first to bring the term into vogue. For Rousseau the capability to perfect oneself distinguishes human beings from non-human animals. However this capability, he held, does not guarantee moral progress; education in the virtues alone could achieve this.

philosophes: A heterogeneous group of French thinkers with a wide variety of intellectual interests, scientific, literary, educational, philosophical, political etc., and with aspirations for social and institutional reform and the improvement of humanity, who became influential at the time of the Enlightenment. They believed in the possibility of human progress, advocated tolerance, and supported the advance of scientific and rational thought, and education. Francois-Marie Arouet, or as he signed himself, Voltaire (1694–1778), was its most influential member, others were Diderot (1713–84), Montesquieu (1689–1755), d'Alembert (1717–83), etc.

Port Royal Philosophy/Jansenists: One of the great schools of the century, the Port Royal school was inspired by the work of Cornelius Jansen (1535–1638), a controversial Catholic bishop and Augustinian theologian opponent of the Jesuits, who was for a time *regius* professor of scriptural interpretation at Leuven. The Port-Royale convent was closed down in 1661 and the community dispersed, but its thinking persevered afterwards in many ways. Jansenist thinking emphasized original sin and the inherent depravity of humanity, hence the necessity of divine grace for salvation, and taught the doctrine of predestination.

positivism: A philosophical school of thought which dates back to Francis Bacon (1521–1626) and the British empiricist school of the seventeenth and eighteenth centuries for which all genuine human knowledge must belong to the observable and experienced, and contained within the boundaries of science. It, therefore, warns against the claims of theology and metaphysics, and restricts the function of philosophy to rigorously examining and explaining the scope and methods of science and exploring the implications of science for human life. Jean-August Comte (1798–1857), in the nineteenth century, sought to extend the methods of scientific investigation into the realm of human behaviour and pioneered sociology.

postmodernism: A word with a largely controversial and indeterminate meaning. Commonly used in scholarly circles to accord with Jean Francois Lyotard's (1924–98) famous definition of it in his book *The Postmodern Condition* (1979), to mark a deep 'incredulity' or distrust of metanarratives, particularly those of the Enlightenment, with which modernity came to age and grew; those of justice, freedom, rationality, and the like.

progressive education: The term 'progressive' was used in the late nineteenth century to distinguish the 'new' methods of teaching from the traditional. Progressive education, like *Emile*, roots education in experience, but, beside Rousseau, it drew much also from Friedrich Froebel (1781–1852), Johann Pestalozzi (1746–1827), and Johann Friedrich Herbart (1776–1845). Other strong emphases were on problem solving, on an integrated curriculum, cooperative learning, learning by doing, and children's projects. A Progressive Education Movement founded in America by Stanwood Cobb (1881–1982) in 1919 continued until 1955.

progressivism: As a general term is linked with an attitude favourable to change or reform, the platform of John Dewey's (1859–1952) educational thinking. Its contrary is traditionalism. Not surprisingly, progressivist educators set their thinking in opposition to the traditional curriculum. Dewey, who supported progressivism early on rejected the practice of dichotomising progressive and traditional education in this way later.

social contract: (see state of nature) The concept dates back at least to Plato's time and to the sophist Lycophron. Plato (427–347 BC) himself discussed it, after a fashion, in the *Gorgias* and the *Republic*, but it was brought into the foreground of modern political philosophy by Thomas Hobbes (1588–1679), John Locke (1632–1704) and Rousseau. Its most influential recent version is undoubtedly that found in the liberal political philosopher John Rawls' (1921–2002) book *A Theory of Justice* (1972:1973).

state of nature: Refers to humanity's original state of being before the introduction of civil society; i.e. the state of being absolutely free from laws and moral constraints. State of nature theories were popular in the Enlightenment period, but the first influential theory in politics was Thomas Hobbes' (1588–1679). Rousseau was right to point out that any such a theory must be hypothetical. Hobbes presented a negative picture of the state of nature and held that a social contract which set up civil society was required to redeem humans from the barbaric and desperate state it signified for them. John Locke (1632–1704) and Rousseau presented alternative, more optimistic, views. But Denis Diderot (1713–84), for instance, rightly held that although the study of humankind was a worthy enterprise it was bound to be inconclusive because since there is no one single human type there is no one model of human nature either.

REFERENCES

Baker, B. (2001). (Ap)Pointing the canon: Rousseau's Emile, visions of the state and education. *Educational Theory*, *51*(1), 1–43.

Bertram, C. (Ed.). (2003). *The Routledge Philosophy Guidebook to Rousseau and the Social Contract*. London: Routledge.

Blits, J. H. (1991). The depersonalized self: Rousseau's Emile. *Educational Theory*, *41*(4), 397–405.

Bloom, A. (1991). *Emile or On education*. Harmondsworth, UK: Penguin.

Boyd, W. (1968). *The Emile of Jean-Jacques Rousseau*. London: Heinemann.

Carbone, P. F. (1985). Toward an understanding of Rousseau's educational ambivalence. *Educational Theory*, *35*(4), 399–410.

Compayre, G. (1908:2002). *Jean-Jacques Rousseau and Education from Nature*. Honolulu, HI: University Press of the Pacific.

Cranston, M. (1983). *Jean-Jacques: The Early Life and Work of Jean-Jacques Rousseau 1712–1754*. London: Allen Lane.

Cress, D. A. (Ed. and Trans.). (1987). *Jean-Jacques Rousseau: The Basic Political Writings*. Indianapolis, Cambridge: Hackett Publishing Company.

Damrosch, L. (2005). *Jean-Jacques Rousseau: Restless Genius*. Boston, New York: Houghton Miflin Co.

Darling, J. (1978). Progressive, traditional and radical: A re-alignment. *Journal of Philosophy of Education*, *12*, 157–166.

Darling, J., & Nordenbo, S. E. (2003). Progressivism. In N. Blake, P. Smeyers, R. Smith, & P. Standish (Eds.), *The Blackwell Guide to the Philosophy of Education*. Oxford: Blackwell Publishing.

Dent, N. (1992). *A Rousseau Dictionary*. Oxford: Blackwell.

Dent, N. (2005). *Rousseau*. New York, London: Routledge.

Dewey, J. (1916:1966). *Democracy and Education*. New York, London: Macmillan Publishers.

Dewey, J. (1938:1970). Experience and Education. In S. M. Cahn (Ed.), *Philosophical Foundations of Education*. New York: Harper Row.

Donald, J. (1992). *Sentimental Education*. London, New York: Verso.

Dunn, S. G. (2005). *Philosophical Foundations of Education: Connecting Philosophy to Theory and Practice*. New Jersey: Pearson Prentice Hall.

Durant, W., & Durant, A. (1967). *Rousseau and Revolution*. New York: Simon and Schuster.

Gauthier, D. (2006). *Rousseau: The Sentiment of Existence*. Cambridge: Cambridge University Press.

Gay, P. (1987). Introduction and Notes. In D. A. Cress (Ed.), *Jean-Jacques Rousseau: The Basic Political Writings*. Indianapolis, Cambridge: Hackett Publishing Company.

Gilead, T. (2005). Reconsidering the roots of current perceptions: Saint Pierre, Helvetius and Rousseau on education and the individual. *History of Education*, *34*(4), 427–439.

Gutek, G. L. (2004). *Philosophical and Ideological Voices in Education*. New Jersey: Pearson Prentice Hall.

Hall, S., Held, D., & McGrew, T. (1992). *Modernity and its Futures*. Oxford: Polity Press/The Open University.

Inston, K. (2006). Jean-Jacques Rousseau's 'Post-Marxist' critique of alienation. *Philosophy Today*, Fall, 349–367.

Johnston, S. (1999). *Encountering Tragedy: Rousseau and the Profile of Democratic Order*. Ithaca, London: Cornell University Press.

Kelly, C., & Grace, E. (Eds.). (2009). *Rousseau on Women, Love, and Family*. Dartmouth: Dartmouth College Press.

Kelly, C., Masters R. D., & Stillman, P. G. (Eds.). (1995). *Jean-Jacques Rousseau: The Confessions and Correspondence Including the Letters to Malesherbes*. Hanover, London: University Press of New England.

REFERENCES

Kontio, K. (2003). The idea of autarchy in Rousseau's natural education: Recovering the natural harmony? *Scandinavian Journal of Educational Research*, *47*(1), 3–19.

Lang, L. (Ed.). (2002). *Feminist Interpretations of Jean-Jacques Rousseau*. University Park, PA: Pennsylvania State University Press.

Mason, J. H. (1979). *The Indispensable Rousseau*. London, Melbourne, New York: Quartet Books.

McDonald, C., & Hoffmann, S. (2010). *Rousseau and Freedom*. Cambridge: Cambridge University Press.

Oelkers, J. (2002). Rousseau and the image of 'modern education'. *Journal of Curriculum Studies*, *34*(6), 679–698.

O'Hagan, T. (1999). *Rousseau*. London: Routledge.

Peukert, U. (1999). Early childhood education as a scientific discipline: A state-of-the-art perspective. *International Journal of Early Years Education*, *7*(3), 213–221.

Rawls, J. (1972:1973). *A Theory of Justice*. Oxford: Oxford University Press.

Reisert, J. R. (2003). *Jean-Jacques Rousseau: A Friend of Virtue*. Ithaca, London: Cornell University Press.

Richmond, A. S., & Cummings, R. (2004). In support of the cognitive-developmental approach to moral education: A response to David Carr. *Journal of Moral Education*, *33*(2), 197–205.

Riley, P. (Ed.). (2001). *The Cambridge Companion to Rousseau*. Cambridge: Cambridge University Press.

Roland Martin, J. (1981). Sophie and Emile: A case study of sex bias in the history of educational thought. *Harvard Educational Review*, *51*(3), 357–372.

Roosevelt, G. G. (1990). *Reading Rousseau in the Nuclear Age*. Philadelphia: Temple University Press.

Rorty Oksenberg, A. (Ed.). (1998). *Philosophers on Education*. London, New York: Routledge.

Rousseau, J. J. (1750:1987). Discourse on the Sciences and the Arts. In D. A. Cress (Ed. and Trans.), *Jean-Jacques Rousseau: The Basic Political Writings*. (Rousseau's date of publication)

Rousseau, J. J. (1755a:1987). Discourse on the Origin of Inequality. In D. A. Cress (Ed. and Trans.), *Jean-Jacques Rousseau: The Basic Political Writings*. (Rousseau's date of publication)

Rousseau, J. J. (1755b:1987). Discourse on Political Economy. In D. A. Cress (Ed. and Trans.), *Jean-Jacques Rousseau: The Basic Political Writings*. (Rousseau's date of publication)

Rousseau, J.-J.. (1761:1997). *Julie, or the New Heloise*. Hanover, London: University Press of New England. (Rousseau's date of publication)

Rousseau, J. J. (1762a:1987). On the Social Contract. In D. A. Cress, (Ed. and Trans.), *Jean-Jacques Rousseau: The Basic Political Writings*. (Rousseau's date of publication)

Rousseau, J. J. (1762b:1991). *Emile or On education*. London: Penguin Classics. (Rousseau's date of publication)

Rousseau, J. J. (1770:1953). *The Confessions* (31st ed., A. Bloom, Transl. and introduction). London: Penguin Books. (Unpublished in lifetime, date of completion)

Rousseau, J. J. (1771:1985). *The Government of Poland* (W. Kendall, Transl., H. C. Mansfield, preface). Indianapolis, IN: Hackett Pub. Co. (Unpublished in lifetime, date of completion)

Rousseau Jean-Jacques. (1776a:1990). Rousseau Judge of Jean Jacques: Dialogues. In D. Masters Roger & K. Christopher (Eds.), *The Collected Writings of Rousseau* (Vol. 1.). Hanover: London:University Press of New England. (Unpublished in lifetime, date of completion)

Rousseau, J. J. (1776b:1979). *The Reveries of the Solitary Walker* (P. France, Transl. and introduction). London: Penguin Books. (Unfinished at his death, date of first writing)

Rusk, D. (1918:1979). *Doctrines of the Great Educators* (5th ed., revised by Scotland, J.). London: The Macmillan Press.

Shaver, R. (1990). Emile's education. *Journal of Philosophy of Education*, *24*(2), 245–255.

Simpson, M. (2007). *Rousseau: A Guide for the Perplexed*. London, New York: Continuum.

Soetard, M. (1994). Jean-Jacques Rousseau (1712–1778). *Prospects*, *XXIV*(3/4), 423–438.

Spring, J. (1994). *Wheels in the Head*. New York: McGraw-Hill.

Starobinski, J. (1971). *Jean-Jacques Rousseau: Transparency and Obstruction*. Chicago, London: University of Chicago Press.

Strong, T. B. (2002). *Jean-Jacques Rousseau: The Politics of the Ordinary*. New York, Oxford: Rowman & Littlefield.

Viroli, M. (2002). *Jean-Jacques Rousseau and the 'Well-Ordered Society'.* Cambridge, UK: Cambridge University Press.

Wiborg, S. (2000). Political and cultural nationalism in education: The ideas of Rousseau and Herder concerning national education. *Comparative Education, 36*(2), 235–243.

Wokler, R. (2001). *Rousseau: A Very Short Introduction.* Oxford: Oxford University Press.

Printed in the United States
By Bookmasters